Basic Income

Ideas in Progress is a commercially published series of working papers dealing with alternatives to industrial society. Authors are invited to submit short monographs of work in progress of interest not only to their colleagues but also to the general public. The series fosters direct contact between the author and the reader. It provides the author with the opportunity to give wide circulation to his draft while he is still developing an idea. It offers the reader an opportunity to participate critically in shaping his idea before it has taken on a definite form.

Future editions of a paper may include the author's revisions and critical reactions from the public. Readers are invited to write directly to the author of the present volume at the following address:

Tony Walter
15 Southcot Place
Lyncombe Hill
Bath BA2 4PE
Great Britain

Basic Income

Freedom from Poverty, Freedom to Work

by Tony Walter

Marion Boyars
London · New York

Published in Great Britain and the United States in 1989
by Marion Boyars Publishers
24 Lacy Road, London SW15 1NL
26 East 33rd Street, New York, NY 10016

Distributed in the United States by
Kampmann & Company, New York

Distributed in Canada by
Book Center Inc., Montreal

Distributed in Australia by
Wild and Woolley Pty Ltd., Glebe, NSW.

British Library Cataloguing in Publication Data

Walter, J.A. (Julian Anthony), *1948—*
    Basic income: freedom from poverty,
    freedom to work. — (Ideas in progress).
    1. Personal income.   Distribution.   Theories
    I. Title   II. Series
    339.2'2'01

Library of Congress Cataloging in Publication Data

Walter, J.A. (Julian Anthony), 1948—
    Basic income.
    (Ideas in progress)
    Bibliography: p.
    Includes index.
    1. Income.   2. Basic needs.   I. Title.   II. Series.
HC79.15.W34   1988   362.5'82   88-16707

ISBN 0-7145-2882-X Original Paperback

Typeset in Baskerville 11/13 and Helvetica by Ann Buchan (Typesetters), Shepperton
Printed and bound in Great Britain by
Biddles Ltd, Guildford and King's Lynn

Contents

Note on terminology   6
Introduction   7
1. The Crisis   11
2. What is Basic Income?   18
3. Historical Sketch   23
4. Who Pays and How Much?   34
5. The Incentive to Work   48
6. The Reasons Why   57
   i   Simplicity   58
   ii   Preventing poverty   62
   iii   Two ethics   77
   iv   Automation   88
   v   Liberty   95
   vi   Equality   107
   vii   An independent income for women   116
   viii   An independent income for those
               needing care   128
   ix   Social cohesion   132
7. Ideology   142
8. Conclusion   153
Bibliography   157
Notes   159
National Contacts and Archives   170
Index   171

Table 1. One Possible Basic Income Scheme   41
Table 2. Basic Income Guarantee 1(a): net incomes   46
Political Ideologies: A map   149

In North America, *social security* refers to government-funded pensions and health insurance for the retired and disabled, to which anyone who has paid the required contributions is entitled. *Welfare* by contrast refers to benefits that are available only if your income falls below a certain level; that is, they are income-tested. In Western Europe, the official term *social security* is used much more widely to cover all cash benefits, and informally *welfare benefits* is also used in this wide sense; *the welfare state* extends to services in kind, such as health care and social work. It will be clear from the context in which sense I am using these various terms. In Europe, *social assistance* is the equivalent of the American *welfare* or income-tested cash benefits. In the UK, social assistance has been largely in the form of *supplementary benefit* but since April 1988 has been modified and renamed *income support*. The *marginal tax rate* is the amount of each extra pound or dollar earned that is lost in income tax or lost benefits.

Basic income is the only way that modern societies can prevent poverty, without at the same time inhibiting liberty and enterprise. In this book, I explain why.

The economic system of the West, based on the paid job, does not ensure material security with dignity for every citizen. The basic contract of our economy is that each household provides at least one paid worker who supports the other individuals in the household. This support comes either from the earner's present wages or through pension and other social insurance entitlements built up through past earnings. Thus the basic economic needs of each citizen are supposedly guaranteed.

This contract, however, is breaking down:

- High levels of unemployment are tacitly accepted by governments.
- Increasingly, households consist of two or more workers on the one hand, or none at all on the other. The single-earner household is becoming a thing of the past.
- Social security in many countries is largely funded by earners from other contemporary households rather than by the accumulated contributions of past earners. This has led to hostility from earners toward certain classes of welfare recipients.
- There is evidence that income is often not adequately transferred within the household to dependent members.
- To be dependent for economic support upon either another member of the family or the state is associated with low status in a society that sees dignity only in a paid job.

- Increasingly in several countries, social security payments are income-tested, thus making it not financially worthwhile for recipients to strive to increase their earnings.

With the paid job failing to provide every citizen with basic material needs, many European countries have witnessed in the 1980s increasing interest in an alternative concept. This would provide a basic income[1] for each man, woman and child, irrespective of whether they receive earnings or other income. Such a scheme would phase out as many reliefs and allowances against personal income tax, and as many existing social security and other state-financed cash benefits, as practicable; and replace them with a basic income paid automatically to each and every individual man, woman and child.

Allied with other policies, I argue that basic income would help to

- Prevent poverty at source
- End the poverty and unemployment traps
- Foster enterprise among the lower paid
- Improve conditions for collective bargaining by low-paid workers
- Give women and other former dependents more autonomy
- Give everyone more freedom to choose their own mix of paid and unpaid work, leading to new and more flexible patterns of work
- Create a less divided society.

People often respond to this radical idea in one of three ways. One response dismisses the idea out of hand: 'No-one would ever want to work again! They'd all retire to Florida and society would collapse into decadence.' A second response is equally cut and dried, embracing basic income as a wonderful idea which would immediately solve every problem under the sun; the instant convert then sets about trying to convert all his or her friends without having begun to consider any of the complexities. A third response is to consider basic income a nice proposal for some as-yet-unattained affluent, automated utopia, but hardly feasible just now. I believe all three responses to be naive. The resulting debate is often less than fully informed.

This book sets out the case for basic income as a thoroughly realistic option for the 1990s. The real limit is not whether a basic income scheme would work, but whether people want it. This book therefore is devoted mainly to answering the question '*why* basic income?'. There is a surprising number of enthusiastic answers to this question, from a wide range of people, groups, interests and philosophies. This is one of the strongest points in favour of basic income, since a proposal with such wide ramifications and effects would have to hold at least some appeal for capitalist and socialist, woman and man, earner and non-earner, if it is ever to be implemented and then not be abolished with the first change in government.

I have kept figures and statistics to a bare minimum. I know this will be unpopular with some experts, but there are two good reasons. First, I want the book to be read by those who are not at ease with tables and graphs. Second, figures from one country may be difficult to understand and of limited value to readers in another country. Throughout, reference will be made to more detailed studies into which both enthusiasts and critics may dig for detailed statistics.

Writing this book has been far from a lonely business, with encouragement, interest and constructive criticism coming from many quarters. I would particularly like to thank The Basic Income Research Group; those whose hard work, vision and efficiency enabled the First International Conference on Basic Income to take place in Belgium in September 1986 at which many useful contacts were made; also those who, true to the spirit of American hospitality, laid on seminars and interviews when I visited the USA in October 1986, in particular John and Judi Ayers, Sheldon Danziger, Irv Garfinkel, David Moberg, Charles Sackrey, Jim Weaver and Tony Carnes; and those who read and commented on all or part of the first draft of this book — Peter Ashby, Andrew Hartropp, Geoffrey Hubbard, Bill Jordan, David Lyon, Anne Miller, Hermione Parker, Fred Twine, Philippe Van Parijs,

Robert van der Veen, and Philip Vince. The thoughtfulness and detail of their comments have been really appreciated, even if it has meant that rewriting has become a rather more lengthy business than usual! I also gratefully acknowledge financial and personal support from the Joseph Rowntree Charitable Trust. And last, but never least, thank you to Diana Barlow for once again typing cheerfully and near flawlessly.

Basic income has most to offer those who find themselves without an adequate income and who find themselves trapped into poverty; it also helps those on low incomes. This book is for such people. It is also, however, for those many who are comfortably off and who have a sense of responsibility for those whom fate in our society has treated less kindly. Many of the comfortably off are unhappy with the amoral attitude to economics so fashionable today and are searching for practical ways to foster a more just and more caring society. Basic income offers such a way.

Chapter One

The Crisis

Enterprise *and* welfare?

When I visited North America in 1986, I witnessed the puzzling spectacle of charitable food banks being set up in almost every town because people did not have enough to eat, at the same time as hundreds of farmers in the mid-West were going bust because they were producing too much food. In a society that had more food and other goods than it knew what to do with, I found expert after expert who rejected the idea of basic income or indeed any other expansion of public welfare, not least because their country 'could not afford it'! It was as though the economic system could not cope with abundance, but was hooked on scarcity. Something clearly is wrong both with the economic system and with the welfare system, and more importantly something is wrong with the interaction between the two.

Time was when at least some societies believed in the possibility of both wealth and welfare. The Beveridge Report of 1942, blueprint of the British welfare state, aimed for 'freedom from want' while at the same time optimistically asserting that 'The State, in organizing security, should not stifle incentive, opportunity, responsibility; in establishing a national minimum, it should leave room and encouragement for voluntary action by each individual to provide more than that minimum'[1]. In the 1980s, however, influential critics in several countries assert that this hope was unfounded, that welfare saps enterprise to a disastrous degree and that the chief losers are the poor themselves. The thinking of Professor Patrick Minford in the U.K., and of Charles Murray in his book *Losing Ground* in the USA, has acted as a catalyst that has changed the public agenda so that some governments now believe welfare cuts to be not only good news for the better off who fund them but also good for the recipients[2]. These critics argue that welfare payments erode the freedom not only of the rich but also of the poor, and are ultimately a threat to civil order and family life.

There are significant holes in this critique of the welfare state, not the least being that the countries with the highest welfare spending, such as Sweden and Austria, also have some of the highest rates of economic growth[3]. But the defense of the welfare state is at present nothing like as coherent as the attack upon it, not least because there manifestly are things wrong with the welfare state. It is costing more and more, yet there are still glaring gaps in provision; claimants feel oppressed by, and consumers are rebelling against, the know-it-all paternalism of the professionals and bureaucrats who run welfare services; and the stress on rights seems to have shot itself in the foot, with taxpayers who fund the services and the staff who run them demanding their rights, while the supposed beneficiaries — the sick, the elderly and the poor — find their rights come very much at the end of the line.

What then is the way forward? For Murray and others, the problem essentially is that welfare (cash payments, help in kind, special incentives) is offered only to certain citizens, usually those in most need. This encourages them to stay in need, and encourages others to get into the state of need that will qualify them for the carrot of welfare. Murray advocates the abolition of all welfare, leaving people with just the stick of poverty which will force them to stand on their own feet and make good. Sticks work better than carrots, because carrots induce people to line up to claim them.

There is a certain logic in this extreme position, even if you consider it flawed thinking. The other position of extreme logic is that, if giving welfare carrots to only some of the people causes problems, and it undoubtedly does, then give the carrots to everyone! This is the thinking behind the universal free education that all modern societies take for granted, and behind the National Health Service, free for everyone at the point of access, that is popular both in the UK and some other countries. Far from inhibiting personal enterprise, it is widely believed that guaranteed health care and basic education are essential if individuals are to lead full and independent lives.

This is also the logic behind basic income. If everyone receives a basic income, then no-one will choose to be idle in order to qualify for benefits, and all may earn without fear of losing benefits. This was seen clearly by Lady Juliet Rhys-Williams, one of the early proponents of the social dividend, writing in 1942:[4]

'How, then, is the policy of providing freedom from want, to which the Nation is committed in the Atlantic Charter, to be carried out, while retaining the profit motive as the mainspring of industry, and shunning all the expedients of Government compulsion to which we have become so inured during the war, but shall detest so heartily in the days of peace?

The solution to the problem seems to lie in the abandonment of the strange convention, derived from the old ideas of private charity, that the State must on no account assist any of its citizens unless they are either destitute or sick, and the substitution for it of the democratic principle that the State owes precisely the same benefits to every one of its citizens. On this basis, if assistance is to be given to any, it must be given to all, and since maintenance payments are essential for the sick and unemployed, then they must also be granted to the employed and healthy.'

In this view, income support from the state should not *replace* hard work and enterprise, but lay the basis for it.

The longer view

The issue is not a new one. Any civilized society will ensure the basis for subsistence with dignity to each household. How this is done typically depends on the basic economy of the society.

In peasant societies, the key is for each household to own or have unfettered access to its own plot or plots of land. Where this is not so, as in many parts of the world where the peasants' land has been stolen from them by military imperialists, by western-style plantation capitalists, by local landlords (as in Britain in the enclosure movement), or by state collectivization (as in the Soviet Union in the 1930s), then people become either demoralized or impoverished, or both. Selling your own land during famine in order to buy food is also a tragically common path to destitution. Village-based collectivization has some-times been successful, but typically it is laws enabling household ownership of land that are the main bulwark of peasant civilization. Many Third World countries today are enacting precisely this kind of land reform. Thomas Jeffersons's vision also was of a free society of small farming households owning their own land. And as far back as Ancient Israel, the Jubilee law parcelled out the promised land equally to each household, ordering any land subsequently sold to be restored to the original household every fiftieth year; this aimed not only to prevent destitution but also to maintain the land upon which Israelite family and clan life were based.

In industrial societies, most people have left the land. Paid employment replaces land as the basis for subsistence, though only a tiny minority of millionaires have so much money that they can do without household members performing unpaid housework and childcare. Each household hopes to contain at least one wage-worker, or to benefit from the pension or other insurance paid for over the years by a wage-worker. The governments of civilized industrial societies aim at full employment, and organize or encourage insurance paid from earnings as the guarantee against loss of earnings.

This goal, and its associated paid work ethic, are widely pursued by the middle and working classes of industrial societies, with only a tiny but perhaps significant minority of intellectuals, hippies and sub-employed youth raising questions about it. Questions must be raised, however, for — despite its popularity — the goal of one-plus earner per household does not guarantee subsistence with dignity for anything like the entire population, and is possibly less effective than the Jeffersonian or Jubilee systems in attaining this goal. We may not be as civilized as we think.

Although most *households* receive earnings or an earned pension, only a minority of *individuals* earn: 46% in the USA, 43% in the UK, 35% in Holland, 30% in Ireland. The rest are denied the opportunity (through unemployment, sickness or gender discrimination) or the right (through youth or old age) to earn, and some have chosen not to earn (usually in order to raise children or pursue further education). These non-earners are supported chiefly by their spouse, by relatives and by tax-payers, and suffer certain deprivations.

Firstly, there can be poor individuals within affluent households; children and wives may not be given enough by the head of the house to live with dignity. About one in three women in Britain who divorce and live off minimum state benefit find themselves better off than when they had been living with a husband typically earning substantially more than that minimum[5]. Many more who do not divorce, along with their children, remain in poverty within officially non-poor households. As Anne Miller[6] has put it, a beggar in a rich society is still a beggar.

Secondly, economic dependents typically have low status in the eyes of society and often in the eyes of their own families. Housewives, the unemployed, children, old people, the sick, the disabled — the list of economic dependents is a pretty accurate list of those who have little status. Old people like to feel loved by their children, but survey after survey shows they do not like to be financially dependent on them. Much the same is true of students vis-a-vis their parents. And the ambivalence of non-earning housewives about their dependent status is a major theme in twentieth century economic and family history.

Thirdly, the unpaid work of financial dependents, especially that done by wives for husbands and children, is typically taken for granted, unlike in peasant societies where strength and health to be a productive worker is a major source of status for a woman in the marriage market, and where husbands see wives (and indeed children) as co-workers rather than as dependents. We may have protected women and children from slave-driving men, but in the process their labour has lost any remaining public esteem.

The contract between the household's chief breadwinner and (usually his) dependents therefore does not guarantee subsistence with dignity for each individual. Nor is the contract between government and citizens watertight. Western governments adhered to full employment policies during the buoyant 1950s and 1960s, promising that never again would they allow a recurrence of the Great Depression of the 1930s. But as unemployment has crept back, so governments have abandoned policies of full employment even if their rhetoric tries to hide this. Citizens are not fooled, though. Unemployed claimants ask themselves why they should seek paid work when there is none available, so the contract between government and claimant, that benefit may be claimed only by those seeking work, breaks down. Promises, whether by government to foster employment or by claimants to seek it no longer mean anything, words become devalued, and the moral fabric of trust and integrity, upon which any economic fabric must be built, deteriorates.

At their best, recent workfare programmes in the USA are an attempt to restore the contract between government and citizen, in which the claimant's promise to take any work offered is matched by the state's promise to provide work, paying at subsistence level. However, workfare does not help the majority of welfare claimants who are not in a position to work, still less dependents *within* households.

Some people argue that we are moving into a *post-industrial era* in which automation and phenomenal increases in productivity will all but eliminate full-time paid jobs of the kind we know now. I myself remain agnostic as to whether we are in fact moving in this direction; I don't find crystal-gazing a terribly exact science. However, we are fools if we do not at least take seriously the *possibility* of an end to the industrial era. To continue to base social status on a wage if only a minority of households, still less individuals, can command a wage will be as archaic as to base status on land ownership in an era in which few households own land. If the basis for subsistence with dignity for the peasant household is land-ownership, and for the industrial household is the wage, then what will it be in a post-industrial society in which jobs will be as scarce as land now is?

Some argue for a basic income for each individual so that a post-industrial society can offer subsistence with dignity for all. Others argue for basic income now as a remedy for industrial society's flawed guarantee of subsistence through a paid job; the work ethic needs supplementing. Work patterns have to become more flexible, perhaps with more part-time jobs, if the economy is to thrive; but many workers fear this threatens their living standards. The material security of basic income could give individuals and households the confidence to explore the new ways of working that a dynamic economy requires.

Chapter Two

What is Basic Income?

Basic income would be paid to each man, woman and child, as individuals; payment would not be conditional on other income or lack of it, nor on willingness to work, nor on gender. It would be paid to all those currently domiciled in a country. The level of basic income would vary by age, replacing pensions and child allowances, with supplements for those without other income or who incur extra living costs. This system would replace social security and welfare payments, and personal tax allowances and reliefs as far as is practical. Income tax would be paid from the first pound, dollar, franc or mark of extra income, but the basic income itself would not be taxable. Separate national insurance or social security funds would be abolished. The unit for both basic income and income tax would be the individual rather than the nuclear family.

For those earning, or those with unearned income, the individual's net income would be BASIC INCOME *plus* OTHER INCOME *minus* INCOME TAX ON OTHER INCOME. In practice, the basic income would be deducted from the tax due, as a tax credit. For individuals without other income, basic income would be paid by monthly or weekly cheque. For part-time workers paying less income tax than the value of their basic income, the excess of basic income over tax could either be paid as a supplement in the wage packet, or by separate cheque. For children, basic income could be paid direct to the parent who cares for the child, as with child benefit today in the UK.

Proponents of basic income have one or both of two aims. 1) Those in the 'basic income' tradition are looking to prevent poverty, as opposed to relieving poverty after it has struck.

2) Those in the 'social dividend' tradition are more concerned with the distribution of the nation's wealth. They argue that a person's prosperity depends on membership of a prosperous society as well as on personal effort or talent, and therefore a civilized society should distribute the dividends of prosperity not just to those who succeed in earning or who have special needs but also as a national dividend to all citizens.

Basic incomes for certain groups of people already exist in many countries. Canada, Switzerland, Denmark and Holland give basic pensions to every elderly citizen, whatever their work record. Beginning with Belgium in the 1920s, several European countries provide a child allowance to each and every one of its children. The UK Enterprise Allowance Scheme, already mentioned, provides a basic allowance to eligible individuals starting up their own business, ensuring a measure of security that enables risk-taking by the new entrepreneur. In the USA, the States of Wisconsin and Texas are experimenting with a child support scheme, whereby divorced parents automatically receive $3,000 per year if they are caring for dependent children, partly paid for by an extra tax on the absent parent.[1] Basic income involves extending coverage from these specific groups to the entire population. In the UK, this would mean extending child benefit and various other benefits into a 'citizen benefit'.

Although not named as such, basic incomes already exist in various nations' social security systems; there have also been official proposals for a small basic income to be incorporated into the tax systems of certain countries. The proposal of the UK government in 1972 for a tax credit system would have provided a partial basic income for taxpaying families, by replacing personal allowances with small tax credits. This proposal, however, retained the household rather than the individual as the unit of taxation, and required citizens to be either in paid employment or seeking it. In 1985, the Netherlands Scientific Council for Government Policy recommended a basic income scheme.

Even though basic incomes could not provide an income sufficient to meet everyone's living costs, they are still 'basic' in the sense that they automatically go to every domiciled person and provide a basis on which an adequate income can be built through earnings, support from kin, or a relatively small income-tested benefit. They are still, in the French phrase, *une allocation universelle*, a universal grant — unlike the highly selective tax exemptions and welfare benefits which currently predominate.

Negative income tax

Basic income must not be confused, as it often is, with negative income tax. Negative income tax proposals are like basic income in that they collapse social security and income tax into one, but the philosophy is very different. Whereas basic income is paid universally to each and every individual, negative income tax proposals would give money only to poor households. Such proposals would give poor households an income in proportion to their actual poverty, i.e. it is paid selectively only to those who are absolutely destitute and in proven financial need. This payment is called a 'negative' or 'reverse' income tax. As the poor household's income rises, the negative tax is gradually removed until a breakeven point is reached where the household starts paying positive tax.

Basic income can never be withdrawn and therefore provides a platform onto which individuals can add their own earnings. But negative income tax payments are progressively withdrawn as a household betters itself, and can be said to reduce the incentive to work hard and earn more.

Negative income tax payments would be made to the household rather than to the individual. Because the aim is to meet financial need, and no more, the incomes of all household members have to be taken into account and an assessment of household need made. Otherwise, negative income tax would be paid to the non-needy wife of a millionaire, or the layabout husband of an heiress. With basic income, this is not a consideration since individuals receive their basic income on account of their being permanent residents, in much the same way as Queen Elizabeth II received family allowances for her four children for so long as they were under 18 without, apparently, anyone objecting. Negative income tax proposals assume that the head of a household passes on a fair share of any payments to dependents within the household. When this does not happen, such payments are not well targeted at the poorest individuals. Basic income, by contrast, gives equally to every member of every household.

These main differences between basic income and negative income tax are of basic philosophy, but there are also technical problems peculiar to negative income tax. In most countries, income tax is calculated on a yearly basis, whereas income maintenance programmes have to operate on a monthly (USA) or weekly (UK) basis if they are to respond to poverty which inconveniently does not announce itself a year ahead to those struck down by sickness, disablement or unemployment. This means that negative income tax returns would be due monthly, creating an administrative burden for the tax authorities (though perhaps no more than income maintenance officials currently endure). It would be particularly cumbersome for those whose earnings vary monthly, weekly, or even daily. Those who move in and out of jobs frequently, those who work different hours from one week to the next, and the self-employed are precisely the kind of flexible worker that many, especially right-wing, governments are trying to encourage. It is paradoxical that negative income tax advocates are usually on the Right, yet their favoured scheme would be a nightmare for their hero: the flexible, enterprising person trying to lift him or herself out of poverty by taking work whenever and wherever available. Basic income, in contrast, does not vary with varying income. Basic income schemes can, moreover, provide supplements for people whose basic living costs are higher, such as the very old or those with a disability. Negative income tax schemes have difficulty coping with such variations.

Advocates of negative income tax argue that these problems can be overcome with computerization and/or with carefully varied tax rates. Further, some negative income tax proposals work out in practice like some basic income packages, and, where basic income provides the only income of a household, some basic income proposals would have to be supplemented by something rather like a small-scale negative income tax. So, although there are the major differences in principle I have described, it is also important to look closely at the practical details of any actual scheme.

Chapter Three

Historical Sketch

What is the history of the idea of basic income? There are several strands in several different countries, some of the strands leading nowhere, some leading to related ideas such as the negative income tax, and some leading to the basic income as it is now being widely discussed. Without going into eighteenth and nineteenth century thinking on the subject[1] I will sketch some of the more recent precursors of basic income.

Social credit

Industry in Britain expanded during the First World War in order to sustain the war effort, and one Major Clifford Douglas was amongst those concerned with how this productive capacity could be consumed after the war; would there not be overproduction and unemployment? As an engineer, Douglas could see the enormous productive capacity of industry and was not convinced that citizens would have the spending power to consume it all. For him, the problem lay in the way the banks created credit. He proposed instead social credit. He argued that what backs the value of currency is not the banks, but the productive capacity of the people, and therefore credit ultimately derives from, and is due to, the people.

Although Douglas' ideas were widely known in Britain, they had little influence here. In 1933–4, however, he went on a world tour to Canada, the USA, New Zealand and Australia. On the Canadian prairie in the midst of the Great Depression, he found receptive audiences; a social credit party was formed in Alberta and in 1935 won a landslide victory in the provincial government election. However, one province alone could not change the whole monetary system of Canada; the Alberta social credit party, having also taken on board Douglas' personal stress on freedom and individual responsibility, quickly degenerated into a rather aimless conservative party which continued in power until 1971. British Colombia, rather ineffectively, had a similar social credit government from 1952–72, and there was also political interest in New Zealand. By the late 1930s, Douglas' paranoia about the banks had led him into anti-Semitism, and he lost much of his personal following. Nowadays, even educated Canadians have little if any idea of what social credit originally entailed, knowing it only as the 'funny money party'.

Douglas was one of several intellectuals in the 1920s and 30s who was wrestling with the role of the banks and the causes of economic recession, but his proposed solution was overtaken by Keynesianism and has never been accepted by mainline economists. However, his vision of the problems to be encountered by a post-industrial society may yet prove to have some substance in them[2].

Social dividend

By the late 1930s, the term 'social dividend' was beginning to be used. Oskar Lange used it to refer to the direct distribution among citizens of profits accruing to state-owned enterprises under socialism, although in his original proposal the dividend was proportional to a person's wage and therefore very different from a basic income[3]. As yet, no Communist or non-Communist country disburses dividends from national-ized industries in this way.

In Britain, Lady Juliet Rhys-Williams, an independent economist, published privately[4] what she termed a 'social dividend' alternative to the Beveridge Report. Unlike Beveridge benefits which went only to certain adults without paid work, the social dividend would be paid to every individual man, woman and child in the country. Lady Juliet argued this was the only way to prevent poverty without undermining either personal effort or the dignity of women. Her social dividend would be offered conditional on recipients being in paid employment, seeking it, or keeping house; it was to be offered to individuals so that the housewife as well as the breadwinning husband would have an independent income.

Lady Juliet's proposal lost out to the Beveridge scheme, but she succeeded in taking social dividend out of the hands of utopian cranks and placing it firmly on the map. It was referred to by the economist James Meade in his 1948 book *Planning and the Price Mechanism*, and Meade has been influential in bringing the idea down to the present generation of would-be reformers of tax/welfare[5]. In both Britain and the rest of Europe, there are few surveys of all the various options for reform that do not at least mention social dividend and Lady Juliet.

Guaranteed annual income

Her idea also crossed the Atlantic. It was taken up by the Office of Tax Analysis of the US Treasury during World War II, which included the young economist Milton Friedman, who was later to promote the idea of negative income tax in the 1960s. The '60s saw the War on Poverty, with American politicians eager for grand new plans to eradicate the newly discovered scourge of poverty. In true American fashion, a problem had been discovered, and they were damn well going to fix it. To my European eyes, the range of high-level debate at that time about how to fix it is impressive, with top level conferences on guaranteed income schemes among the business and church community as well as among politicians, social workers, and economists[6]. Economists argued for a selective negative income tax, while social workers argued for a universal child benefit along European lines. The economists won, and persuaded President Nixon to put before Congress a Family Assistance Plan which was a negative income tax for families with children akin to the Family Income supplement introduced in Britain around the same time. This failed to gain Congressional approval, partly because welfare advocates feared it would be a cut price scheme and that the money would go to the father and not the mother, partly because conservatives feared it would undermine work incentives. So it scared both conservatives and liberals; the appeal to one camp put off the other, and vice versa[7]. The upshot was a lengthy series of experiments to determine the effect of negative income tax on incentives; the results were ambiguous and in any case the programme took ten years, by the end of which life had moved on.

It had moved on in three ways. One was that the old American mood of distrusting grand federal government programmes had reasserted itself, crystallized in the election of Ronald Reagan to the presidency in 1980. Another was that various partial negative income tax programmes had, under various names, crept in the back door in the early 1970s anyway: i) Food stamps, now worth about $750 per year per person, reduced by 25 cents for every dollar earned, provide a family of four with a guaranteed income of $3,000 and are not removed entirely until household income reaches $12,000. Though administered separately from the tax system, this is in fact precisely the kind of low-level negative income tax that Milton Friedman had been arguing for. ii) Medicaid provides help with medical expenses, depending on your income. iii) The Earned Income Tax Credit provides a credit against tax for the working poor. Another development was that poverty among the old had been largely eradicated by a generous state pension scheme plus Medicare which gave the impression of being insurance-based but in fact re-distributed substantially to the elderly poor.

These developments illustrate enduring themes in American attitudes to income support. The help provided for the poor of working age was earmarked for food (foodstamps) and health care (Medicaid); taxpayers did not want to see Americans starve or be unable to receive medical attention, but they were not happy about giving money unconditionally to the poor to spend as they pleased, as Friedman had wanted. Cash help *was* provided for the elderly who, it was felt, deserved it[8].

An unconditional basic income was never on the agenda. Democratic presidential candidate George McGovern mentioned a partial basic income called credit income tax[9] in his platform in 1972, but was insufficiently briefed and was so embarrassed by people laughing at the idea of a handout for Rockefeller and other millionaires that the idea was quickly dropped.

The MacDonald Commission

If the climate in the USA was hardly conducive to basic income, things were different in Canada, which had developed a social security system along more European lines. The MacDonald Commission on the Canadian economy, reporting in 1985, came out strongly in favour of a Universal Income Security Program (UISP). In its 'Option A', the personal income tax exemption would be abolished; each adult and the first child of a single parent family would receive a guaranteed annual income of $3,825 and other children $765, which would guarantee a family of four an income of $9,180. This would be topped up by income-tested local benefits, providing an annual guarantee of $13,000.

An interesting feature of this negative income tax proposal is that only 20 cents are removed for every dollar earned. This means that UISP will be available to families up to an income of $45,000 (approximately £22,000), which includes well over half the population. (Median earnings were $15,000 in 1985. Median household income was $28,000, and $38,000 for a household of 4–5 persons.) A negative income tax that benefits well over half the population is in practice pretty close to a basic income[10].

The MacDonald Commission was set up by the long-standing Trudeau Liberal government, but by the time it reported the Conservatives had got into power. They dismissed UISP as too grandiose, while the NDP left-of-centre opposition complained that UISP was too stingy[11]. This is not the first time, and certainly will not be the last, that radical reform of social security has been opposed by the left because it was not pitched high enough in the first instance, and opposed by the right for the opposite reason. It is easy to see why piecemeal reform is usually the order of the day; if and when basic income comes onto the political agenda, its proponents will need political ingenuity as well as carefully worked out and costed programmes.

United Kingdom

In 1972, Edward Heath's Conservative government put forward a tax credit scheme[12], which would have replaced tax allowances for employees earning more than £8 per week and also would have covered some social security beneficiaries. Personal tax allowances were to be replaced by tax credits, cashable in certain circumstances where they exceeded any tax liability. This would have provided a sort of basic income for a significant proportion of the population, but also with significant gaps such as most part-time earners. There was debate as to the method of payment of child credits. There was criticism from the left that most of the credit went to non-poor families[13]. This is an inherent feature of tax credit, universal benefit, and basic income schemes; in retrospect, the criticism seems beside the point, for what matters for the poor is how much they receive not how much others receive[14]. By 1974, a Labour government was in power, and that was the end of that, although Labour has never formally rejected the principle of tax credit or basic income. Had the Conservatives got back in 1974, Britain would now have a limited basic income system of sorts, capable of expansion and improvement. What we have actually inherited from this affair is a very limited basic income for children, in the form of child benefit.

The tax credit proposal was still there in the 1979 Conservative election manifesto, but by 1986 it had been definitely rejected by the Conservative Chancellor of the Exchequer both on grounds of cost and because the Conservatives are committed to 'the distinction between reward for effort and support for need, between what individuals gain for themselves and what they receive from the State'; in other words between earnings (good) and state handouts (bad)[15]. However, ministerial interest has been for basic income.

Through the 1970s, a Conservative back-bencher, Sir Brandon Rhys-Williams, son of the Liberal Lady Juliet, had been doggedly pursuing his mother's social dividend idea and providing a trenchant critique of the Conservative philosophy just quoted. His research assistant, economist Hermione Parker, meticulously costed various basic income options[16], which were presented to a parliamentary committee in 1983. This committee, reviewing the whole area of income tax and income support, was clearly interested in both Hermione Parker's proposal and a tax credit proposal put forward by Philip Vince in 1979. Rejecting comprehensive negative income tax schemes because of their high marginal rates of tax on those with low incomes, the committee strongly recommended in its final summing up that the government do a feasibility study of basic income and tax credit schemes[17]. At the time of writing (1988), the government has shown no public sign of doing this.

Working from a very different angle, namely his identification as a socialist with unemployed claimants, social worker Bill Jordan from the University of Exeter had been exploring the social dividend idea which he had first encountered in the radical Claimants Union in the early 1970s. In 1984 he met Hermione Parker and a few other interested individuals, among them Philip Vince, Anne Miller, a feminist economist, Keith Roberts, atomic physicist, and later Peter Ashby, ex-Trades Union Congress, and together they set up the Basic Income Research Group (BIRG). The aim was to investigate and consult to see whether a basic income would in fact be practical in the UK. They still hold seminars, inviting representatives of various sectional interests to explore the implications, while Hermione Parker continues her costing exercise, discussed in more detail in the following chapter.

The Liberal Party had meanwhile adopted Vince's tax credit plan[18], which included a basic income component supplemented by a negative income tax which overall imposed an 84% marginal tax rate on the poor. This was better than the over 100% rate that currently afflicts some of the working poor in the UK who lose £1 or even more out of each extra £ earned, but some advocates of basic income felt it must be possible to do a lot better than that.

The Social Democratic Party had by 1982 proposed a negative income tax with a very high tax-back rate. By the summer of 1986, the SDP and Liberal Alliance had stated in print that their scheme 'provides the foundation for developing into a basic income scheme'[19]. This is the first time I had come across basic income affirmed positively in a policy document of a major British political party.

The UK Green Party, very marginal to national politics

compared to some European green parties, is however like several of its European counterparts including basic income as a key plank in its economic and social policy[20]. The National Union of Students now advocates a basic income for youth. Some may dismiss this as a student fantasy, but it is worth remembering that the students of today are the leaders of tomorrow, and they are being familiarized with the idea. The Labour Party is still generally wedded to revamping the old Beveridge social insurance-based scheme, possibly together with a national minimum wage, while the young bloods on the Conservative right advocate negative income tax[21] and/or workfare[22]. The influential Institute for Fiscal Studies published in 1984 a plan for a comprehensive negative income tax[23]. Basic income is not yet on stage at Westminster, but it seems waiting and ready in the wings.

The Road to Louvain-la-Neuve

The Netherlands have seen considerable debate on basic income in the past ten years. The pattern of debate is not unique to Holland: introduced on a moral-emancipatory plane by scientists and Christians, rejected by others as utopian, followed by serious interest by certain organizations as the recession deepened, followed by a major and careful report, followed once again by dismissal from the two major political parties[24].

It started in 1975 with J.P. Kuiper, a professor of social medicine. He was concerned about alienation at work, and began to think about disconnecting labour and income. He read Robert Theobald's *Free Men and Free Markets* which had been influential in the USA in the 1960s, and began speaking about the emancipatory possibilities of an unconditional income. He aroused interest in ecological and Christian left circles but hostility from unions and employers wedded to the desirability and inescapability of paid labour.

By the early 1980s, however, unemployment was rising and the Voedingsbond FNV, the union of food workers in the largest Dutch trade union confederation, embraced the idea. The Royal Institute of Engineers (KIVI) the small radical party PPR and the slightly bigger (left) liberal-democratic party D'66 were also enthusiastic. And a lively debate has been taking shape inside the Labour Party (PvdA), which is Holland's largest party.

1985 saw the debate move on from the kind of society that a basic income could help bring about to a pragmatic discussion of technicalities. On behalf of the government, the Netherlands Scientific Council for Government Policy (WRR) produced an advisory report[25], recommending a partial basic income. In tone and argument, the document reminds me of Canada's MacDonald Commission. The partial basic income would be topped up by a general insurance against loss of earnings and a residual general assistance scheme, and voluntary supplementary insurance is also encouraged. The report fell on deaf ears in The Hague, however, for the government was at that time concerned with controlling expenditure with tighter means-tested benefits. We may conclude that 'the basic income is not yet an item on the political agenda in Holland, however likely the issues it raises have been, and are, discussed'[26].

Scandinavia is currently extremely prosperous, with generous social security and very low unemployment, which led one sympathetic Norwegian to comment in 1986 'Maybe basic income is the solution, but what's the problem?' Although the Swedish Metalworkers Union has demonstrated interest[27], Gunnar Adler-Karlsson has commented 'Like Norway, and unlike Denmark, we Swedes are realists and do not discuss things of this sort!' It is in Denmark that most interest has been shown within Scandinavia, chiefly through the writing and speaking of Adler-Karlsson and the publication in 1978 of Niels Meyer's best-selling *Revolt from the Center*[28].

Other European countries contain isolated individuals or the odd organization that is interested, such as the West German Green Party, the Irish Transport and General Workers Union, and the French Unemployed Union[29]. The Youth Forum of the European Communities has published a document advocating basic income and is actively debating it. There is a move in the European Parliament, chiefly from Greens, to get basic income onto the agenda. The European Commission is continuing to show interest.

Belgium, however, in particular the Collectif Charles Fourier at the University of Louvain-la-Neuve, has provided a focus for international work on basic income. The Collectif has amassed an impressive holding of publications, and in 1986 organized and hosted the First International Conference on Basic Income, to which seventy delegates came from fourteen European countries, with several being turned away for lack of space. This conference revealed for the first time how diverse people in diverse countries and for diverse reasons have independently arrived at the concept of basic income. The conference demonstrated that interest in basic income comes not only from every quarter of the political spectrum, from nuclear scientists and feminists, from right wing economists and left wing sociologists, from trade union officials and the unemployed, but also that this breadth of interest is at least potentially there in several European countries. Following the conference, the Basic Income European Network (BIEN) was formed to provide a focus for this continuing interest.

Chapter Four

Who Pays and How Much?

Typically, in Britain at least, experts respond to proposals for social security reform in one of two ways. One goes: 'I cannot respond to your proposal until you put some figures on it. Only then can I know whether it benefits poor people or whether the government can afford it. How much will it take from the rich and give to the poor?' The other response points out that, especially with modern computers, you can make any system — whether social insurance, basic income, negative income tax, or whatever — be more or less expensive, more or less redistributive. What matters is the principle behind the proposal, and whether that principle is one which ordinary people believe in, because only then will they be willing to be taxed to fund the scheme or even be willing to claim benefits from it.

Although I have a personal inclination towards the second response, it seems to me that both approaches, detailed figures and realistic philosophy, are necessary. It is necessary to know our philosophy of life and what people see as ethical and un-ethical, before we can state objectives and the conditions that must be fulfilled to meet those objectives. Then we will have the parameters within which a particular scheme can be devised and costed. It is highly unlikely, for example, that a centralized command economy such as the Soviet Union would consider a basic income scheme which would further the personal autonomy of the individual citizen. At the same time, it is important to know that some kind of basic income scheme can be devised in which the sums add up, before it is worth discussing either the principles involved or the kind of society basic income might help promote. In particular, it must be demonstrated that basic income can provide at least the same level of income support as do present tax and social security without unreasonable extra expenditure. Fortunately, this has been done, by the Dutch WRR report, by the Canadian MacDonald Commission and, most detailed of all, for the UK by Hermione Parker.

In this chapter, I will raise some of the difficulties in costing basic income schemes, and give some details of one particular option. Grounding the discussion in some idea of what is actually possible is essential before we later explore the philosophy and possible economic, social, personal and moral consequences of basic income.

How much to pay?

A basic income designed to meet basic living costs must be based on some idea of what basic living costs amount to. Several countries, including the USA, have an ongoing tradition of surveys measuring what people need to live on, with welfare benefits pitched at a proportion of this minimum (usually below it!). Britain, however, is in the curious position of currently spending £44 billion on cash benefits to relieve poverty, yet the last known attempt to calculate how much is needed to keep different kinds of families out of poverty was made by Sir William Beveridge in 1942![1] At the moment, costed basic income schemes for the UK have used current social assistance scales as their starting point rather than what it actually takes to live in the UK; Parker is therefore hoping to commence a major survey on precisely this question.

The problems in determining basic living costs are enormous. Some people need a car to get to work, others do not. Some frail old people and car-less mothers of young children live next door to the cheapest supermarket in town, others living on peripheral housing estates cannot manage the two bus-rides to the supermarket and have to use the only remaining, and often vandalized and expensive, local shop. In Britain, by far the biggest single factor in the cost of living is the cost of the roof over your head. The price of the cheapest available housing can vary from nothing or a few pounds for someone who has paid off their morgage, to £30 per week for public housing, to £100 per week for a mortgage for a young couple in Greater London. Wildly variable housing costs in Britain render a simple basic income scheme impossible, just as in the 1940s they had rendered impossible the pure social insurance scheme Beveridge had wanted.

In the USA, people are more willing (and able) to move away from high cost areas of the country, but there is a vast difference between those who have health insurance largely provided for them by employers or Medicare/Medicaid and those — usually the working poor — who have to pay their own medical bills. Just as basic income in the UK cannot cope with high housing costs, so no basic income scheme in the USA could possibly cover everyone's medical bills. Basic income could only be an option in the States when there is universal coverage, one way or another, of the bulk of people's medical bills. Though the USA is not likely to develop a national health service along British lines, the numbers of uncovered people is steadily decreasing and it seems likely that in the next few decades the patchwork of employer and state schemes will add up to universal coverage.

Another factor still causes wide variations in several countries. In Finland and Sweden, there is a universal right to the fruits of the forest, so even poor rural folk have free fish and game which makes nonsense of a national minimum for either current welfare benefits or for basic income. A very large minority in Ireland have smallholdings, and in the UK even some city people grow all their own vegetables on rented allotments. There is also a large difference in the USA between gardenless northern slum dwellers and the rural poor of the South. Not every household in these countries has moved at a uniform pace from the grow-your-own peasant economy to the buy-it-all industrial economy, and indeed some ecologists are trying to reverse this increasing dependence on money.

These variations in living costs suggest that a basic income pitched at a uniform level sufficient to meet the full living costs of every citizen, including the disabled and gardenless resident of an expensive city, is quite out of the question. It could even add up to more than the total gross national product of the nation! And even if it were by some miracle affordable, would it be just? For, while enabling most of us to live in luxury, it would barely provide enough for the unfortunate disabled urbanite. A viable basic income scheme would therefore have to be topped up by other income: earnings, unearned income or certain benefits to aid those with unusually high living costs. Examples are Parker's schemes in which there is an income-tested supplement to help with housing costs, and the MacDonald Commission's national universal income supplemented by locally administered top-up schemes.

It is sometimes thought that we cannot afford basic income now, but might at some time in the future when the economy is more affluent. I doubt it. What strikes me as a Briton visiting North America is not only how much more money and things people have there, but also how much more money and things people genuinely *need* there. There seem to be two reasons for this. One is that as a society becomes more affluent, so even an ascetic saint would not be able to declare unilateral independence and continue to live at the material standard of some bygone age without totally isolating him or herself from ordinary social intercourse and obligations. Indeed, isolation is precisely what the Amish communities in the USA have found necessary in order to pursue their pre-industrial lifestyle. In the normal course of events, as affluence increases so people require more goods if they are to remain participating citizens[2].

The other factor is that we are located within an era that was started millennia ago by the invention of money. We are at a moment in time of a long, long process in which human households are moving from producing (or bartering) all their own goods and services to one in which more and more is bought and sold. Looking at more economically advanced societies, I see populations that have moved further in this process towards the cash nexus dominating life. In the USA, most journeys cost money whereas in the UK a majority are still free, being on foot. In Sweden, and the USA, more child care is paid for than in Britain. In the USA, less food is cooked in the household, and more households go out to a restaurant and pay someone else to cook their meals. And, of course, the more urban a society, the less people are able to grow their own food and have to pay other people to grow it. As an old lady from Sheffield, UK, put it, recalling the 1930s: 'Working-class people used to be proud of how much they could do with very little money; now people feel ashamed of how little they can do without a lot of it.'[3] Whether or not you share the judgement that this process is a shame, it certainly is a fact. As a society grows more affluent, so the money people require for ordinary living also grows. A more affluent society can spend more on basic incomes, but people will require higher basic incomes[4]. There is no utopia waiting in the future. Either the sums for basic income add up now, or we abandon the idea.

A scheme for the UK

Is it possible to devise a basic income scheme that is significantly better than the current complexity of income tax exemptions and social security benefits and better than other proposed alternatives? I hope readers will be able to come to their own conclusions about that by the end of the book. For the rest of this chapter, I will outline one particular option that has been proposed for the UK, as an illustration of what a basic income might look like. I cannot stress too strongly that this is only one amongst several possible schemes and I describe it for illustration only.

In order to be taken seriously by any UK government, you have to show that a basic income scheme could have operated in a selected recent year. The proposed system must be revenue neutral, that is, must not cost more than existing social security payments, tax allowances and reliefs. In order to prevent poverty, two further criteria pertain, at least in the UK:
i) Existing distinctions on account of sex or marital status must be replaced by a system which is completely marriage neutral.
ii) There needs to be a double redistribution of income, from rich to poor, and from people without dependent children to people with dependent children.

How much money is there to play with? The basic income replaces social security payments and income tax allowances and reliefs. Social security payments in 1985–6 came to just under £44 billion. Income tax reliefs for the same year were:

	£m
Married man's allowance	12,900
Single person's allowance	7,550
Wife's earned income allowance	3,450
Age allowance	425
Additional allowance for one-parent family	150
Reliefs for:	
Employees' contributions to occupational pension schemes	1,400
Employers' contributions to occupational pension schemes	2,200
Investment income of occupational pensions schemes	3,500
Lump sum payments to pensioners	1,000
Retirement annuity premiums	325
Life assurance premiums	640
Mortgage interest relief	4,750

It would be rash to think that, if abolished, all of these reliefs would materialize as cash in the government's hands, but it is safe to say that the cost of these reliefs approaches the cost of cash benefits. Transfer expenditures in the UK therefore cost around £80 billion in 1985–6. To gain cross-party support, a basic income scheme would have to cost that or less, for in the present political and economic climate, no party is contemplating massive increases in public spending.

Hermione Parker has proposed several basic income schemes for the UK that come within this cash limit. They all operate on the same principle: a basic income with supplements for people with high housing and other costs and for people unable to supplement their basic income by their own earnings. The options vary in the size of the basic income and the way in which the supplements work, but the aim throughout is to provide benefits at least as good as at present for the poorer half of the population and with lower marginal tax rates so that it is easier than at present for the not-so-well-off to add to their net income.

I will illustrate just one of her options, the Basic Income Guarantee 1(a), or BIG 1(a)[5]. This provides a universal grant, sufficient to meet the basic needs of those excluded from the labour force by old age or disability, and less than sufficient for everyone else; they will have to top it up by earnings, help from other family members, unearned income or state assistance with housing costs. The basic income is pitched at the current level of income support (social assistance) for a single non-householder. The elderly and people with disabilities will receive substantial supplements; unlike the fit of working age, they are unlikely to be able to increase their income by their own efforts and deserve a basic income that will enable them to thrive, not merely subsist. Working age citizens who have little or no other income will not be able to live solely on their basic income, so they will also be able to claim housing assistance which would be reduced by 33 pence for every extra pound of other income. (Table 1)

The method of financing[6] suggested by Parker is an income tax of 40% on earnings; there would be an employers' payroll tax of 10%, and national insurance contributions abolished. All in all, this adds up to a tax on earnings comparable to what existed in the UK when Parker devised this scheme. This is possible because of the money available from abolishing most tax reliefs; this will raise the amount of tax actually paid by many of the better off, even though their marginal tax rates may not rise. Such tax rates could well be acceptable in the UK and

Table 1. One Possible Basic Income Scheme,
UK 1984–5: Parker's BIG 1(a)

State earnings related pension, national insurance and all income tax reliefs abolished. Starting rate of income tax 40%. New 10% employers' payroll tax.

	POPULATION NUMBERS[1]	BASIC INCOMES Weekly rate	Annual cost
	m	£	£b
UNIVERSAL BASIC INCOMES			
Each adult	44.0	21.50	49.1
Each child (0–15 years)	12.3	15.00	9.6
BASIC INCOME SUPPLEMENTS[2]			
Each householder	19.9	—	—
Each expectant mother	0.7	15.00[3]	0.3
Each widow/widower	0.3	21.50[3]	0.2
Each lone parent	0.9	12.50(?)	0.6
Each person aged: 65–84	7.8	27.50	11.1
85 & over	0.6	32.50	1.0
Each disabled person	0.9(?)	27.50	1.3
DISABILITY COSTS ALLOWANCE	?	variable	2.0
			75.2

PLUS HOUSING ASSISTANCE: Approx. £7 + rent + rates (local taxes), somewhat less for household headed by someone over 65. Reduced by 33 pence for every £ earned. Would not cover mortgage interest payments; new mortagees would be expected to take out insurance against loss of earning as part of the Building Society contract.

[1] 1982–3
[2] Added to universal basic incomes.
[3] For six months only.
From H. Parker, 'Costing Basic Incomes', *BIRG Bulletin*, Spring 1985, Table 1.

other European countries accustomed to relatively high taxes. In the USA, with its much lower basic tax rate, a different kind of scheme would have to be devised.

With a basic tax rate of 40%, those receiving housing assistance will lose this at a rate of 33 pence in the pound as well as being taxed at 40 pence in the pound. This means they will lose altogether 73 pence of each pound earned up to the point at which they are no longer eligible for housing assistance. This 'marginal tax rate' of 73% for some poor people is higher than anyone would wish, but is less than some people are faced with at present and in the major published alternative reforms. Less than half the number of people that currently need housing assistance would need it with BIG 1(a); this is because the elderly and some other groups are much better off with BIG 1(a).

These figures illustrate what one particular basic income scheme would look like were it to operate in the UK during 1985. In practice, basic income would have to be phased in over a period of years, during which time many factors such as the health of the economy will have changed, together with changes due to the introduction of the basic income itself. Certainly basic income would have many consequences effects. The number of people in paid employment could go up or down. Abolishing relief on firms' pension schemes would surely have major consequences for the stock market and for the financing of British industry and would arouse major opposition. Abolishing relief on mortgage interest would have major effects on the housing market, on the costs of getting to work and on investment patterns.

The scale of such consequences indicates that these reliefs should be abolished gradually. However, this will create difficulties of its own. When a tax relief is abolished, typically what happens is that the previous beneficiaries do not end up paying all the extra tax, as intended by government, but put their money elsewhere so that it qualifies for some other relief. Of course, that would not be possible if all reliefs were abolished simultaneously, but that would lead to chaos.

Furthermore, politics are such that in all likelihood not all tax reliefs *would* be abolished. In the year of writing, President Reagan of the USA has just succeeded in scrapping about half of the 5,000 tax deductions previously available to the American taxpayer and this has been hailed as a great triumph; to abolish the other half is likely to prove impossible. Further, it is likely that in time government will introduce new reliefs for activities it wishes to promote. In sum, in the UK, not all the £80 billion that is theoretically there will actually prove to be there, a potential major stumbling block for basic income schemes.

Expense

Basic income schemes are often dismissed as ludicrously expensive. In the UK, there are about 26 million paid employees, and their basic income would appear as a tax credit, deducted from their tax bill, amounting in Parker's BIG 1(a) to 26m x £21.50 x 52 = about £30 billion per year. The other £45 billion of basic income plus say £2 billion of housing assistance would be paid as a benefit. Under current accounting conventions, this £47 billion would appear as 'public expenditure', while the £30 billion would reduce the tax bill; this would not appear good in comparison with the current £44 billion expenditure on social security and £38 billion reduction in the tax burden through reliefs and allowances.

But this apparent expense of basic income is purely a result of the accounting convention that labels social security as public expenditure and therefore 'bad' and tax reliefs as reducing the tax burden and therefore 'good'. In fact, each reduces the government's revenue, and each is used for the same purpose of helping citizens with low income or with the costs of housing or bringing up a family. Further, the current accounting convention makes no distinction between public expenditure where the government itself actually spends money — on police, school-teachers, roadmenders, soldiers and so on — and transfer payments which the government does not spend but simply passes on from one group of citizens (taxpayers) to another group (claimants) who often are the same people anyway.

Voters will not be concerned with how much money is passing through the government's hands nor with how this is defined by government accountants. They will be concerned with whether they will be better or worse off than before. That is the true measure of expense. How is basic income costed out? For most households, the change in net income will be quite small but inevitably, as indeed is the purpose of any programme designed to attack poverty, there will be a redistribution of income. The extent of this redistribution will depend on the actual figures of an actual scheme, but inherent in basic income are three particular kinds of redistribution and it is difficult to envisage a basic income scheme that does not redistribute in these ways:

The first is that there will be a shift in resources from chief breadwinners to dependents. Basic income would go to each individual, whereas most current social security benefits and tax exemptions go to the 'head' of the household. For many households, therefore, basic income would involve a 'wallet to handbag' shift, and in this sense will be considered expensive by full-time paid workers, especially those who look only at their net wages. But if they are concerned more about the total amount of money coming into the house, as I believe responsible breadwinners must be, then households with below average earnings will find their net household income will have risen. In the BIG 1(a) option, this will also be true for households on somewhat above average earnings with dependent children.

This leads on to a second kind of redistribution, operating over the lifecycle of most citizens. All but those permanently disabled from childhood and those who die in childhood are at some stage in their lives earners, and at some stage dependents. Basic income takes from us while we are earning and gives to us when we are dependent. This is the principle underlying family allowances, free eduction and old age pensions, and most basic income schemes simply take it that bit further.

Thirdly, because basic income is not restricted to those without paid employment, it inevitably helps the low-paid, in BIG 1(a) up to about average earnings (Table 2). This is not at the expense of the non-earning poor, but at the expense of the comfortably off. It is those on above average earnings who will be paying more than now, most of whom are men. It is from these, of course, that politicians, accountants, economists, and civil servants are drawn, and they will be correct when they describe basic income as expensive. It will indeed be more expensive for them than is the present system. But if they imply that it is somehow expensive for 'the nation' or for 'the government', then they are pulling the wool over the eyes of the ordinary voter.

This brings us to an ethical point. Is there the possibility of one group voting in basic income, and another group having to pay? Charles Murray claims the history of welfare reform in the USA in the past twenty years to have been that of an educated liberal elite leaning on politicians to legislate for the working poor to pay for the non-working poor. In one sense, this would occur with basic income. In BIG 1(a), the basic income is roughly equivalent to the married man's tax allowance, so a male breadwinner now also enjoying tax relief against mortgage interest and occupational pension premiums will lose more in tax exemptions than he gains in basic income to the benefit of his children and other dependents who will receive a basic income. That is looking at it from the point of view of the individuals concerned. From the point of view of the entire household, however, families on below average income will gain with this basic income scheme.

Table 2. Basic Income guarantee 1(a).
Net incomes, for one-wage families with 2 children (UK 1984)

| | Net Income £ | |
Gross weekly earnings £	Existing system	BIG 1(a)
0 (rent & rates* £23)	91	103
40 (rent & rates £23)	108	114
60 (rent & rates £23)	106	119
80 (rent & rates £23)	105	126
100 (rent & rates £23)	102	133
125 (rent & rates £23)	108	148
150 (rent & rates £23)	123	163
200 (£15,000 mortgage)	162	190
400 (£30,000 mortgage)	305	297
600 (£30,000 mortgage)	419	391
800 (£30,000 mortgage + £3,000 superannuation)	546	473
1,000 (£30,000 mortgage + £5,000 superannuation)	655	553

* A local UK tax based on value of house.

Adapted from H. Parker 'Costing Basic Incomes', *BIRG Bulletin* No. 3 Spring 1985, table 3. Tables giving details for a wide range of other households are provided in Parker's *Action on Welfare*.

More to the point is the warning given by Milton Friedman[7] that it is unfair and an infringement on their liberty for 30% of the population to pay more taxes in order to fund the basic income that the other 70% of the population voted for! That is one reason why Friedman prefers a modest negative income tax, in which 70% of the tax-paying population pay for the poor 30% who receive tax refunds, which could not come about unless at least a good number of the 70% voted for it. Friedman also argues, however, that a major purpose of his scheme is to increase freedom for the poor; it is arguable *a fortiori* that in a basic income scheme any loss of liberty for the richest 30% is more than compensated for by gains in personal liberty for the poorer 70%.

There is little doubt that BIG 1(a) *could* be funded in the UK. Whether it *will* be, or *should* be, are more tricky questions by far, for they move us away from accountancy to the altogether more confused areas of politics and ethics, to be discussed in Chapters Six to Eight.

Chapter Five

The Incentive to Work

Perhaps the biggest stumbling block for many is that they reckon lots of people would stop work and live off their basic incomes, or at least reduce their work effort considerably. They argue this would a) be morally wrong, and b) so reduce the income tax collected that the funding of the basic income scheme would collapse. I will leave the first, the moral/political question, till later chapters, and consider now the economic question.

Of the various economic changes mentioned in the previous chapter that basic income might induce and that could conceivably destroy the funding of the scheme, the reduction of the paid labour force is the most obvious. It is, for example, why Lady Juliet Rhys-Williams' original 1942 social dividend scheme required participants to take employment offered them and why she later modified the scheme still further in the light of criticism by Professor Meade about incentives[1]. This economic question has to be addressed if we are to believe the previous chapter's claim that a basic income scheme is financially viable. Only then is there any point in examining whether basic income is politically viable or morally desirable.

In considering this question, at however much of a gut level, public and politicians usually focus on the size of the individual's basic income. 'If it's enough to live on, then they'd give up work!' Researchers, however, usually focus on the tax rates, pointing out that in a basic income scheme in any Western European country both the actual tax on earnings and the marginal tax on extra earnings would go down for significant segments of the population, notably the low paid currently in the 'poverty trap', thus raising the incentive to work; at the same time, marginal and especially average tax rates would go up for certain other groups.

The issue of marginal tax rates is also to the point. People's work effort is influenced not only by how much they have already, but also by how much more they will gain by working more. The question is, how do they respond to incentives? Do different people respond differently? How much can a government tax its citizens before tax revenue actually begins to decline?

Theory

The best way to start thinking realistically about how people would respond to a basic income is to ask what you yourself would do. Would you cease work? Would it make sense for your spouse, your parents, your children? If you or they did, what would you do — would you idly sit on your bum all day? If your answer to any of these questions is 'no', would other people respond differently? If you think so, what is the difference between them and you? If your answer assumes 'They are lazy, but I am not!', do you have any evidence for this assumption?

Having answered these questions honestly, we can now explore how economists predict people would behave. How do individuals respond to their earnings being taxed while at the same time (as in some basic income schemes) knowing that they might just get by without earning? We do not need to guess blindly, because with both social assistance and/or the possibility of financial support by a spouse, many people are already in this situation. The main factors that influence people's response is a) whether they *have* to earn, b) whether they are able to do other work of value to themselves or their households should they give up paid work. In general, when taxes rise, married women engage in paid work less, and married men more. There is a consistent pattern that married women are highly responsive to the rate of tax. In the UK, about half the women who have paid jobs work part-time, usually up to the point at which they would start paying tax or national insurance. Under a basic income scheme, in which every pound over and above the basic income is taxed, it seems likely that in the short run those British women currently working part-time would either give up paid work, or maybe decide to work full-time, or might find ways of concealing their earnings. (It is also possible, see Chapter 6 vii, that in the long run women's wages would rise.) Whether or not these responses by married women are desirable or undesirable for other reasons, they are unlikely to affect tax revenues substantially, since part-timers hardly pay any tax under the present system.

When taxes rise, the employed married man may try to increase his earnings[2] either through working longer hours or through negotiating a wage or salary increase, which results in either increased productivity or increased inflation. Given the usual distribution of domestic tasks, the married woman with a full-time job may well bear in mind she will have less time to do housework and childcare if she works longer at her paid job, and her response is therefore less predictable than that of a man who relies on a wife to do the housework. Most employees, however, of both sexes, are not in a position to choose their hours.

Unemployed people currently lose welfare benefits pound for pound if they declare earnings, even if only a few pounds from a part-time job, leaving them in a moral dilemma. Many full-time jobs do not pay enough to make them worth taking. With basic income, unemployed people would not find themselves in this position, for wages would add to, rather than replace, basic income. Financially, it would always be worth earning. If it is true, as some argue, that many jobs paying less than social assistance rates simply are not created, then basic income could generate a considerable number of new jobs.

They would pay badly, but would nevertheless lead to a substantial net gain in income. (See Chapter 6.v)

Bart Nooteboom[3] has argued convincingly that basic income would encourage the setting up of small businesses, acting rather like the UK Enterprise Allowance Scheme: 1) Basic income provides a subsidy for the diseconomies of small-scale production, which often form a barrier in the early stages of production. 2) Wage earners who are dissatisfied because their entrepreneurial talents are lying fallow are currently often dissuaded from setting up on their own because of the lack of income for their family during the formative years of the new business and because of the risk of failure. Basic income would provide a secure base which could encourage risk-taking. 3) The present subsidies and incentives to start up small businesses are complex, often unco-ordinated and often work against each other. Several of them could be scrapped under a basic income scheme. 4) Selective subsidies to those starting a business, such as the Enterprise Allowance Scheme, can create unfair competition to other businesses not eligible for the subsidy. Many women, for example, are not eligible for the Enterprise Allowance Scheme. The basic income would be available to everyone. Universality promotes enterprise, fairness, and a freer market. If these arguments are valid, basic income would lead to more small businesses, and more government revenue.

Basic income would pose a tricky problem in the case of old age pensioners[4] who in the UK can currently earn a certain amount on top of their state pension before being taxed. With basic income, they would be taxed on every pound they earned, which clearly is bad news for those many pensioners who enjoy or even rely on part-time earnings. This is one reason why Parker's BIG 1(a) scheme provides a basic income for the elderly well in excess of the current basic state pension.

Evidence

Since a basic income scheme for all has never been set up, there is no direct evidence of how people would behave under basic income. In the United States in the 1970s, however, four major experiments were made over three and five year periods to explore the effect of a negative income tax on the incentive to take paid work. To summarize many thousands of pages of documentation[5], the result was that during the period participation in the world of paid work declined, more than proponents of negative income tax would have wished but less than opponents had expected. Most of those opting out of paid work were, not surprisingly, married women.

The political and expert response to these ambiguous results was confused. Some argued the decline in paid work effort to be significant (the earnings of wives were believed to be the key that lifts poor families out of poverty), others thought it insignificant (what really mattered was that there was an economic recession at the time and women are always the first to be squeezed out of employment). Some argued that the decline in paid work effort underestimated what would actually happen under a negative income tax (even a five year trial is too short for people to change their working habits), others that it overestimated (the experiments focussed on poor families with a rather loose attachment to the labour market, and excluded higher earners more likely to respond to higher taxes by working harder). Some argued that the decline in desire for paid work was a bad thing (paid employment is the chief way in which people support themselves and their families with dignity), others that it was a good thing (the experiments gave poor black mothers the choice to stay at home to look after their children, and gave those between jobs more time to seek the best job rather than have to take the first offered).

Apart from the unclear results of the experiments, the implications for introducing a basic income scheme, either in the USA or elsewhere, are limited. Negative income tax is different from basic income in several ways described in Chapter 2. And the USA is crucially different from Canada and Western European societies in that it has little income support for the unemployed and considerably less unemployment than several of these other nations. The provision of negative income tax to Americans would give many the hitherto unknown option of moving out of paid work for a while, with consequent labour shortages and decreased tax revenues. In other western societies, however, any jobs released by those opting out would generally be taken up by the unemployed: tax revenues would be maintained, and basic income for those opting out would cost no more than current social assistance for the involuntarily unemployed. Perhaps all that would happen is that involuntary unemployment would be replaced by voluntary unemployment, with consequent better motivation and satisfaction among both paid and unpaid workers.

The only implications for basic income from the negative income tax experiments are what we know already: that those opting out of paid work are likely mainly to be married women or pensioners who may not be paying much tax anyway, and that a few working age males may drop out completely and others take longer between jobs. None of this would have a major effect on income tax revenue under a universal basic income, though under a selective negative income tax paid only to the poor it would considerably increase such payments and threaten the viability of such a scheme. The MacDonald Commission[6] is surely correct that the effects of basic income on tax revenue are trivial, but the political effect of people able to cease paid work at will might very well not be acceptable; the Commission argued that, to gain political support, it might be necessary to make basic income conditional on a test of willingness to take paid work, as did Lady Rhys Williams four decades earlier.

Two European studies on the probable effect of basic income

on labour supply have produced similar results. Ian Walker[7] has predicted a large number of married women would cease part-time paid employment were Parker's BIG 1(a) scheme introduced. Paul-Marie Boulanger predicts that a full basic income in Belgium would initially reduce labour supply by about 12%, falling thereafter to 1.5 to 2% per year[8].

It seems, then, that the simple effect of basic income would be to reduce labour supply significantly, though tax revenues would not decline proportionately since few of those choosing to leave paid work are now paying a significant amount of tax.

That assumes nothing else changes. Many argue for basic income precisely because they want other changes, and it is certainly possible that basic income could be a key plank in a programme for the regeneration of jobs, which could counteract the effect predicted by the above-mentioned studies. The two official reports arguing for basic income (the MacDonald Commission and the Dutch WRR report) are wise to argue for gradual implementation, monitoring the labour supply and tax base consequences as we go. Until such steps are taken, the issue now is not that basic income could not possibly pay for itself, but that many are unhappy about the new choices it would give some people (mainly women, blacks and the poor) and a possible loss of pride for others (mainly male breadwinners). The stumbling block at present is not one of economics but of values and of politics.

Unpaid work

In this chapter I have been concerned with the likely effect of basic income on whether people would give up, or take, paid work and the consequences for how much income tax is raised. A related question is the effect on the incentive to do unpaid work. This too will affect whether a basic income scheme could be financed.

Ray Pahl's classic study[9] of how households organize all their various kinds of work produced two major findings. One is that, just as industry requires capital investment if it is to be productive, so does the private home require capital investment in tools, washing machines, cars, books, guitars, computers, etc, if it is efficiently to produce its own entertainment, washed socks, educated children, well-fed breadwinners, and all the other products of the typical home. Underinvestment due to lack of finance is strongly associated with low activity households. This leads to Pahl's second finding, that it is precisely those households in which there is little or no income from paid employment that do least in the way of unpaid work. Increasingly, there are two Britains: those households with two or more earners which also do lots of unpaid work in and around the home; and those households with no earners, which can afford to do little other than eat and sit in front of a television set. Pahl concludes that a basic income would increase the total amount of work done, by giving no-earner and poor single-earner households that little bit extra income by which they could capitalize hitherto undone activities as well as spend more on basic necessities.

This would generate unpaid work which simply is not done at present, and increase the quality of life for many households. But it would not generate tax revenue to fund the basic income. Another effect of basic income, however, could well release public funds. A lot of the debate about public services (road sweeping, hospitals, etc) seems to assume that society has to choose between getting these services done and paid for by government or by private industry. But there is a third major provider of services, namely the unpaid labour of friends, family and neighbours. In the UK, the Conservative government is emptying psychiatric and geriatric hospitals in the hope that the patients' own families will be able to look after them. This is resisted by many people who might have been willing to look after their loved ones themselves were they given sufficient back up and resources, which currently they are not.

In the USA there is serious concern that middle class wives taking full-time paid work have depleted the charitable good works on which America not only rightly prides itself but also depends, and will necessitate extra publicly funded services.

The basic income could well lead to a resurgence of charitable work. It would mean that young people who want to join Mother Teresa's order or devote themselves in some similar way to the needy would have something to live on. It would mean that more people could freely choose to look after their sick relatives rather than have them looked after in expensive hospitals at the taxpayer's expense or be forced to look after them when they cannot afford to. It might further the process analyzed by Richard Titmuss in his seminal study of the UK National Health Service, whereby recipients of a free gift are themselves more willing to give freely.[10]

Of course, none of this is certain. A penny-pinching government could use basic income to dump public services onto the family and onto charities, without providing any further back-up. But a progressive government that understands there is more to life than gross national product could use basic income to revitalize the relation between voluntary, private and public sectors, with workers in each sector truly being held in high esteem and given adequate support[11].

In sum, a well-designed basic income scheme could increase the amount of work done both paid and unpaid. Crucially, people would *willingly* be in the labour market, or *willingly* out of it; this surely cannot but help job satisfaction, productivity, and human welfare.

Chapter Six

The Reasons Why

I have argued in the previous two chapters that several basic income schemes are financially feasible, and that the key issue is not whether the sums add up but whether citizens want basic income. In this main chapter, I will examine who has advocated basic income and why. One of the intriguing things about basic income is that it has been advocated by people with the most divergent values, political goals and ethical beliefs. More intriguing still, basic income often directly stems from these values, goals or beliefs. How is it that such different starting points can lead to the same concept of basic income?

In each case, others with the same ideological starting point strongly disapprove of basic income; I will discuss their objections and assess whether the objections have substance. In the penultimate chapter, these objections to basic income will be summarized, and then in the final chapter the prospects for basic income sketched.

A good number of people are attracted to basic income in the first instance for neither ethical nor ideological reasons but because of its simplicity. For anyone who has tripped over, or got bogged down in, the complexity of the tax and social security arrangements of their society, basic income comes like a breath of fresh air.

Advantages of simplicity

An obvious advantage of simple integrated tax and social security is that it saves on administration. At present in the UK, it costs 1.25 pence to collect £1 of tax, and 5 pence to give out £1 of benefit. That may not sound much until you realize that many people have much of their benefits taxed away. Consider someone earning £90 per week who pays £15 in income tax and national insurance contributions and receives £17 in benefits such as child benefit, housing benefit and family credit. The net benefit to that person of £2 costs £1 to administer![2] The thousands of civil servants operating the currently separate tax and social security systems might object to a basic income scheme that renders many of them superfluous. The advantage to everyone else, however, is manifest. And even civil servants prefer a simple reform to a complicated reform, if reform there has to be.

A second advantage is that everyone will be able to understand a simple basic income. At present, the rich can afford accountants to get them the best deal out of a complicated system, but the poor cannot. Yet it is often the poor, facing the poverty trap where tax and social security interact in the most illogical and obscure ways, who most need to understand the financial consequences of their own decisions, yet are least able to.

Not only will this clarity enable more people to make rational decisions about their individual lives and to maximize the well-being of their families, but it will also enable them to vote more responsibly. The obscurity of most affairs of state makes it difficult for even informed voters to understand the actual pros and cons of an issue, and indeed politicians themselves are often flying by the seat of their pants because the dials are too difficult to read. In a simple basic income system, the relationship between the level of basic income and the tax rate can be made clear. Anne Miller argues that the level of basic income could be made the subject of a regular referendum.

Finally, the simplicity of basic income could gain votes. The 1986 Reagan tax reform had widespread support, partly because Americans were fed up with each year having to consult 45 pages of instructions and 184 pages of notes in order to fill in their 30 page federal income tax return. Simplicity appeals.

Disadvantages of simplicity

Despite these advantages, however, I do not consider simplicity an important reason for changing to basic income. Why?

First, simplicity may not be a vote catcher. Many citizens do not want to know how much of their tax is going to the poor, to blacks, to single parents or to other people they disapprove of, especially if these people are not required to seek paid employment. One reason that old age social security in the USA over the past twenty years has been so successful in helping the aged poor is that most Americans do not understand how redistributive the scheme is. They are pleased that old people are no longer in such poverty, but at the same time they like to believe they are paying into a fairly straightforward state pension fund for their own old age. The problem of poverty in old age has somehow been solved at no personal cost to themselves, rather like British citizens experience the national health service as 'free'! People vote for pain-free solutions to social problems, whereas basic income is too upfront about who pays for what.

Secondly, I concluded in Chapter 4 that we are talking about a basic income scheme which for those without earnings would have to be topped up by income-tested help for (in the UK) housing, (in the USA) medical costs, or other special needs. This could be much simpler than what we have already, but it is not as simple as enthusiasts sometimes imagine on first encountering basic income.

Thirdly, it is almost certain that, as with Beveridge's social security system for the UK in the 1940s or Reagan's US tax reform of 1986, any basic income bill will not get enacted in its entirety. We will not get as simple a system as some had hoped. And even if by some miracle an entire basic income scheme were enacted, over the years accretions will inevitably accrue and what was simple will end up complicated, as with Beveridge whose grand scheme for ending want is now supplemented by over forty income-tested forms of social assistance! These accretions will occur because the needs of people in poverty are too complex and varied to be resolved by one scheme. There will always be need for residual social assistance, which over the years could well grow like Topsy. New special needs will emerge (for example, neither Beveridge nor the architects of Aid for Families with Dependent Children in the States could anticipate the massive growth of single parent families) which it will surely be deemed cheaper to meet by some new income-tested scheme than by expanding basic income. Professor A.B. Atkinson of the London School of Economics is sceptical of basic income for this reason. I myself do not see this objection as a reason for rejecting basic income, but it is a reason for not proclaiming simplicity as its chief merit!

A final objection to the simplicity of basic income, sometimes made by government ministers, is that the objectives of taxation and of social security are entirely different, and to unite them into one simple system will only lead to confusion. The purpose of taxation is to raise public revenue. The purpose of social security is to relieve poverty and/or to maintain income during periods of loss of earnings. The two systems overlap, and therefore should be properly co-ordinated, but never be integrated into one system and one department.

This does not seem to me to be a reason for refusing to integrate taxation and social security. There are, after all, schemes and government departments with more than one aim. Furthermore, government departments typically compete with each other, and it is an extreme optimist who holds out hope for real co-operation between two separate government departments, at least in the UK!

One thing is clear. Simplicity is not, nor should be, an over-riding *aim* of either taxation or social security. I can easily devise a simpler system than basic income if that is the sole aim — one which raises no revenue and pays no benefits! No, simplicity is a highly desirable *condition* of taxation and social security. Basic income's simplicity is a strong point, but it is not *the* point. Basic income must meet other goals for it to have any credence.

In Britain and in some other countries, basic income is intended to replace the often ineffective existing measures against poverty. Seminars on basic income in Britain attract chiefly those active within the poverty lobby — representing the old, those afflicted by unemployment or disability, children, the low paid and other people vulnerable to poverty. Few of these organizations are definitely persuaded of the merits of basic income, but all are very aware of the de-merits of the present system and keen to explore alternatives such as basic income.

There's a hole in my bucket

How do people in modern western countries stay out of poverty? A main way, of course, is through their own earnings, though it was pointed out in the first chapter that only under half of the population actually have earnings of their own. The second main way of subsisting therefore, is through the earnings of kin, most often a spouse or parent. This, however, does not guarantee adequate subsistence for all individuals: a) Many wives and some children receive less than enough from the male breadwinner in the household. b) For divorcees, maintenance settlements are often not honoured, not least because in the UK, USA and some other countries the absent husband knows that the wife will be bailed out by social assistance. c) In the UK, not all parents pay their student offspring the amount that is assumed by the authorities and deducted from the student grant, thus leaving the student short. d) Although financial help from kin other than spouses and parents is important for many people, this source of help is declining — both because elderly people increasingly do not like to be supported financially by their children, and because in many western countries laws compelling or assuming support of parents or more distant kin have been repealed. In Third World countries where the extended family of maybe thirty to one hundred people is the basic unit, there may exist informal obligations for the better off to support anyone in need within the family, but in western societies where the small nuclear family of mother, father and dependent children is the basic unit there is often nobody else with more income than the person in need.

Henry, or more often Henrietta, therefore finds that there are holes in her bucket which never seems to be able to hold enough to meet basic needs. Modern western governments have tried to plug these holes, in four ways.

The first is through personal tax exemptions or allowances, which let earners off paying tax on the first slice of income. This helps many households, but also has some bizarre consequences: a) With a progressive income tax, which rises for the better off, fixed personal exemptions benefit you more the higher the rate of tax you pay. b) Those who are not earning do not receive the benefit of exemption. In other words, those who least need help get the most, and those who most need help get none from tax exemptions. c) There is no guarantee that the value of the exemption will be passed on to the person in the household who has to pay the bills, often the wife.

Basic income involves replacing the personal allowance with a tax credit. Tax is levied on all earnings, and the basic income deducted from the tax bill; or for non-earners, it is paid in cash. This removes the problems inherent in the personal allowance.

The second prong of the current defenses against poverty is state-arranged insurance against loss of earnings, which is what Americans mean by 'social security'. Bismarck was the first to organize social insurance, in Germany in 1889, and he clearly had in mind not the relief of poverty but earnings-related pensions that would reinforce the work ethic and buy off discontent from workers. West German social security is still strongly oriented to replacing a proportion of earnings. In the USA and many other countries, however, social security has not been run on strict insurance lines and has been used to top up the pensions of those who would otherwise be below the currently accepted poverty line.

Social insurance is a less than effective way to deal with poverty: a) Relieving poverty is not the main aim. b) Over the many years between payment of contributions and claiming, customs may have so changed as to make a nonsense of the criteria for eligibility. The Beveridge social insurance scheme of the 1950s assumed that wives did not earn, and many wives today who have earned for many years find themselves disqualified from certain pension rights because the scheme had no place for them. c) Several benefits require contributions to have been paid in a specific previous year for benefit to be paid this year. It is often a lottery whether the claimant did in fact work and pay contributions during that year. d) Not all the poor are eligible for insurance benefits. They may have a paid job, so earnings have not been interrupted, but the job has never paid enough to lift them out of poverty. Or they may have no earnings, but are ineligible for insurance benefit because they have never earned; those disabled since childhood and the young unemployed are barred for this reason.

To make up for these deficiencies in social insurance, a third system has been expanded, namely a safety net of social assistance (UK: family credit, income support; USA: AFDC, food stamps), to assist those whose income has fallen below a certain level. These income-tested benefits have one or more of three historical foundations. In the UK, USA and the Commonwealth, they may derive from the old Elizabethan Poor Law, which predates social insurance by three hundred years, and whose indignities social insurance was intended to end. Or they may have been developed piecemeal to make up for deficiencies in social insurance. Or thirdly, there are proposals such as Friedman's negative income tax or the 'benefit credit' scheme proposed by the UK Institute for Fiscal Studies[1] which would sweep away all previous income-tested benefits and replace them by a single negative income tax, actually paying the non-earner.

The problem with all such income-tested schemes operating to date is that, because they are paid for by earners and available only to non-earners (or occasionally low wage earners), they carry for many claimants and would-be claimants considerable stigma. This means that not everyone who needs the benefit applies for it; many of those who do feel angry, baffled or defeated by the system; and taxpayers who themselves may be hardly better off feel resentful.

As these programmes have expanded, so the stigma has gone for some, which in turn leads to new problems. Some critics believe there are not enough people making efforts to get off benefit and some people deliberately get themselves in need in order to claim it! For those devoted to supporting their family, it is indeed rational and caring to go for benefits rather than a wage if the family can get more that way, although it is debatable how many actually face this situation. Whatever the actual balance of these phenomena, there is no doubt that few are happy with the expansion of income-tested programmes. Certainly the claimants are not. Sixty year-olds who have scrimped and saved all their lives for their old age find their meagre savings have debarred them from social assistance and are confused and angry that cherished lifelong values are despised by authority. Younger claimants who find benefit reduced by earnings pound-for-pound or dollar-for-dollar have an incentive either to remain idle or become deceitful. A whole folklore among some claimants emerges as to how to beat the system, usually illegally. (Contrast better-off taxpayers who can pay accountants to beat the system legally.) Decent citizens, devoted to supporting their families, are dismayed to find it both rational and caring to go for benefits rather than a wage if their family is to make ends meet.

The manifest limitations of both social insurance and social assistance do not apply, however, to a fourth protection against poverty, *unconditionally* given to certain sectors of the population, irrespective of whether they need financial aid or whether they have paid contributions. This is the kind of benefit envisaged by the minority report (by Sydney and Beatrice Webb among others) of the 1905 UK Royal Commission. The Commission rejected the income testing of the old Poor Law; the minority wished to replace it with unconditional benefits based on citizenship but the majority verdict opted in favour of social insurance, which in fact became the basis of the British welfare state. Nevertheless, unconditional benefits have played a part, both in Britain and elsewhere (but not in the USA). Examples are the British child benefit, the basic state pension in Canada, Denmark, Switzerland and Holland, and certain benefits for disability in some countries. These grants are unconditionally available to those of a certain age or with a disability, and provide basic incomes for these particular sectors of the population.

Basic income

Just as in the children's song, these various attempts to plug the hole in Henrietta's bucket are (apart from the unconditional grants) in some ways self-defeating; the claimant goes round in a circle only to find that there's still a hole or two in the leaky bucket and gets trapped below what most people would deem an acceptable standard of living. This problem is now well-known to both left and right.

Most experts on social security argue for a careful expansion of the four approaches already in existence, retailoring them as new needs and defects emerge. This incrementalist philosophy is challenged by a few on the right, such as Charles Murray, who would like many benefits eliminated so that the main bastion against poverty will not be government programmes but the initiative of the individual. When pushed, however, these critics usually back away from completely demolishing welfare.

Basic income expands the unconditional approach by replacing all tax allowances and social security with an unconditional grant for everyone. It may sound wildly utopian to some, but so did universal free education to many Americans in the 1860s, and a National Health Service to many Britons in the 1940s, not to mention the Webbs' ideas in 1905. The advantages of basic income, over present arrangements are:

i) It forms a base on which everyone who can find a way of earning will be able to benefit from earning. It does not discourage industriousness or saving in the way income-tested benefits do.

ii) Like education in the USA or the health service in the UK, it is available equally to everyone and there is no stigma. Everybody will take advantage of it and indeed will automatically be included in the scheme.

iii) Because it is available equally to everyone, it does not induce anyone into a position of need in order to be able to claim it.

iv) Because everyone receives it, nobody will be left without income. In this sense, basic income does not attempt to plug the holes, but provides a brand new bucket without any holes.

Last year I stumbled across the new bucket principle when visiting the African country of Zimbabwe. Following the thirteen year civil war, many homeless and displaced persons ended up squatting around the capital Harare. A European or North American approach to this problem would have relied on personal initiative and the free market to build houses, and then the government would have bailed out the remaining homeless by building public housing to a comfortable standard. This would of course have been expensive and might also have induced dependence. Instead, the government is building simple two-room basic concrete dwellings for everyone, with sufficient space around each not only to grow vegetables but also for families to extend the dwelling on their own initiative. If you go around this township now, you see a variety from the basic dwelling to three room houses to palatial bungalows, all with the basic dwelling as the core and all maintained with pride. Thus basic, universal provision provides the foundation for enterprise, initiative and dignity; selective provision risks inducing dependence, stigma and dishonesty.

Another surprising result of basic income is that, though given to everyone, it is better targeted on the truly poor than is any alternative. Income that accrues directly to the chief earner (wages, tax exemptions, social security benefits paid through the wage packet, social security based on past contributions) he often considers to belong to him rather than to his dependents and so it is up to him what he does with it. Even income-tested benefits targeted at the poorest households often do not hit the target, namely the poorest individuals within those households. Because they are assessed on the needs of the *household*, they are usually paid to the head of the household, with little or no guarantee that they will be distributed equitably within the household[2]. A basic income, universally allocated to all *individuals*, certainly hits the target.

Henrietta's story

I'll sketch now the traps and dilemmas a real life English Henrietta has found herself in, and how her situation would be transformed by a basic income. Her position is by no means extreme and is typical of many single parents and unemployed in the UK and the USA, and in several European countries too.

Etta was training as a teacher when she met and married Jim. She gave up her training to emigrate with him from the UK, but this did not work out and they returned to England. She did various clerical jobs until she gave up work in her mid-twenties to have her two children. During this period of financial dependence, she discovered she could not trust her husband to give her an amount each week, even though he had a job on a fixed salary. Some of the major bills, such as the mortgage payments and heating bills, he said he'd pay, and she'd only find out he hadn't when the electricity was cut off and she would have to persuade the electricity authority to give them more time to pay. Budgeting became impossible. Things went from bad to worse, and as their second child was being born, Jim left her.

She was now eligible for supplementary benefit (similar in her case to the American Aid for Families with Dependent Children), and for the first time in years was able to budget, plan and take control of the household finances. (As indeed was her right: 'Henry' or 'Henrietta' derives from old German, meaning 'house ruler'!) A good manager, with a friendly bank and holidays and other help in kind from her by no means affluent parents a hundred miles away, she struggled through with dignity to bring up happy, well-mannered and adequately clothed and fed children. Though she did not like being dependent on the state, she valued having more independence and more control over the life of her home than ever she had with Jim.

During this time, she went to court several times to try to enforce the maintenance payments over which Jim was dragging his feet. Since these would have been deducted from her supplementary benefit, she would not in fact have been better off in the short run, but she knew that without the maintenance payments she would find it very difficult ever to get off state dependence and start work. Unqualified, and in the market only for poorly paid clerical work, she was in the unemployment trap, in which a wage would be virtually nullified by lost benefits. Eventually, after three years and Jim facing prison if he prevaricated further, a cheque for £1000 arrived, enough to keep the bailiffs away from Jim for a while so he could procrastinate further. In future, her supplementary benefit would be reduced accordingly.

In the meantime, however, her younger child had just started school and in the hope that maintenance might arrive, she looked for and found a clerical job paying about what she had been getting on supplementary benefit. Normally, this would have been topped up by Family Income Supplement, an income-tested benefit to help families on low wages, but the FIS authorities assumed that she was receiving maintenance from Jim, so she was barred from receiving FIS. She had not in fact received a penny from Jim since the one-off arrears cheque. Being barred from FIS meant she was also not eligible for free school meals for the children, nor for certain other benefits. She was once again living with unpredictability and finding it impossible to make rational decisions that would maximize the well-being of her family, this time not because of an erratic breadwinner but because of a bizarre and opaque set of government regulations. She was fortunate that her parents were now retired and had moved nearby, and a good neighbour looked after the children for the two hours after school before she got back from work; but even being charged only half the going rate by the neighbour this cost more than she really could afford. Overall, she reckons she's about 15% worse off now she's actually wage-earning.

She was surprised to find that she really enjoyed going back to work, and over the next year or two there is the chance of promotion. The key question, though, is whether she will survive financially until that promotion comes. The answer is yet to be seen.

In the meantime, she had an awkward question. She used the £1000 to pay off a bank overdraft. She feared that she would be required to repay the supplementary benefit authorities the value of the maintenance, but this would involve reducing her net income so much that she might well have to give up the job and go back on benefit, precisely the outcome the sup-plementary benefit rules are supposed to discourage! She wondered whether she could get away with not telling the authorities about the cheque — it might be breaking the law, yet it would be in both her interest and theirs that she keep quiet and remain at work. She was troubled by the prospect of being dishonest. Eventually, a relative anonymously asked the authorities about the position. Etta was relieved to hear that she does not have to repay the money, unless she should ever re-apply for social assistance. But the anxiety was real enough while it lasted.

What emerges clearly out of Etta's story is the failure of the various means of support — earnings, kin, tax allowances, and welfare benefits — to interact in such a way as to encourage rather than threaten Etta's initiative, sense of responsibility and good humour. Millions of intelligent, responsible people in the western world find themselves in the same unhelpful kind of situation. How would basic income have changed Etta's life?

When married and living with Jim, hers and the children's basic income would have given her some money with which to plan at least the basics of a household budget. It might have given Jim an excuse to give her even less, but she'd willingly have traded that for predictability.

When divorced, it would have given her and her solicitor more incentive to press Jim to pay maintenance, and Jim less excuse not to, since maintenance would be in addition to basic income, rather than instead of social assistance.

When the younger child started school, she could have taken paid employment in the knowledge that earning would add to the family's income, not subtract from it. Moreover, she could have planned the family's finances because she'd have been able to work out precisely the net benefits from working.

Finally, basic income would not have placed upon her the moral dilemma about whether or not to tell the authorities about her maintenance cheque.

In sum, basic income would have enabled her, while living with her husband, to rescue the family finances whose demise contributed to the divorce; had he left, basic income would have enabled her to become truly the new head of the household, the ruler of her own house. It would have provided dignity, autonomy and meaningful citizenship — both outside and inside her own home. Though basic income is often dismissed as utopian, it is in fact far more realistic about the contemporary reality of living on the edges of poverty in the west than are the often archaic assumptions behind current tax, social security and welfare legislation.

Objections

What are the main objections to basic income replacing tax allowances, social security and welfare payments as the way to attack poverty?

i) A common objection is that people may rely on basic income rather than earnings to support themselves. Especially in the United States, but widespread also in Europe and the UK, there is the feeling that a family should as far as possible lift itself out of poverty by its own efforts. Government should provide not handouts but a framework in which more paid jobs can be created, together with education and training. Some of those on both left and right who have been campaigning for more jobs somehow feel that basic income undermines their efforts.

This fear is understandable, but misplaced. I hope I have made it clear by now that basic income is not intended to replace earnings, but to provide a realistic framework for those for whom earnings are not sufficient, a framework which provides security while at the same time rewarding earning. Running 100 metres is much easier when you have a solid floor under you than a swamp or a floor that begins to collapse the faster you run. Basic income could well go hand-in-hand with employment creation, education and training programmes.

By itself, more employment will not solve the problem of poverty, for some of the households on the lowest incomes at present in the UK and the USA are those with a full-time earner. Generating more jobs does not prevent poverty if those jobs do not pay enough to live on. Some, therefore, argue for a national minimum wage or, in those countries already with such a minimum, to increase it. However, in those countries such as the UK where for many low paid households there is a poverty trap in which they lose, net, as their gross earnings rise, raising wages to a minimum level will leave many poor households as badly off, or even worse off, than now! A national minimum wage would make sense if action is taken to remove this kind of poverty trap, which is exactly what basic income does. For those, surely most of us, who wish to increase the value of the hard-won earnings of the low paid, then basic income is an ally, not a foe!

The other problem with putting all your eggs in the full employment basket is that not all households are able to raise themselves up by their own efforts. Some heads of households are handicapped, physically or mentally, some have babies, elderly parents or sick relatives to look after. Such people may be partly able to support themselves by part-time or unskilled work, but often find this impossible under present welfare arrangements. Basic income, by contrast, enables some of them to have at least some stake in the world of paid employment.

ii) Another objection is that there will never prove to be enough money in the public kitty to pay for an adequate basic income, and therefore more help can be given the poor by carefully identifying needy groups and funnelling funds in their direction. Aware of the problems associated with income-tested benefits and the inadequacy of insurance for those who have not been able to pay sufficient contributions, these proposals usually rely to some extent on what are effectively basic incomes for particular circumstances — for childhood, for disability, for maternity leave, or for widowhood. In the UK, for example, the Child Poverty Action Group has consistently pushed for a substantial increase in the value of child benefit as a key part of their anti-poverty package. Far from opposing basic income, this approach could possibly be one way of moving eventually toward a basic income for every citizen.

iii) Another objection is that universal benefits, such as the UK child benefit, have not maintained their value as well as have tax exemptions. The electorate would be fools to pay more tax simply to receive a handout in the form of basic income. It will turn out to be a bad bargain both for taxpayers who will find themselves paying through the nose, and for dependents who will soon find basic income not enough to live on.

Lawrence Mead, of the Department of Politics at New York University, argues against welfare benefits that do not require recipients to work or seek work. He considers that the expansion of welfare benefits in the 1960s and 1970s as a *right* of poor people, has 'left them in the position of petitioners, dependent on society's goodwill, as anyone is who possesses only rights. . . . The real weakness of welfare recipients today is that they have run out of the obligations that they, like other people, need in order to justify claims.'[3] The value of these benefits has not been maintained, precisely because the recipients are simply petitioners. Advocates of workfare, in which claimants have to work enough hours at the minimum wage to 'earn' their benefit, argue that this will generate the political will to maintain or even increase benefit levels. Society will help those who show willing to do their bit. 'To establish further claims, the poor and their advocates must assert new obligations. They should accept, rather than resist, the new bureaucratic requirements, especially work tests. If more welfare mothers worked, their claim to support would be fundamentally stronger. . . . A focus on obligations is much more likely than continued one-sided claims to rights to justify further benefits for the poor.' Some advocates of basic income, such as Lady Rhys-Williams, James Meade, and the MacDonald Commission, have expressed doubts about an unconditional benefit on precisely these grounds.

This objection appears to have considerable force. However, historical evidence to the contrary is also available. Occupants of the Victorian English poor house were obliged to work, but lost all political rights. So did slaves in the USA[4]. The non-earning wife today is obliged to keep house for her breadwinning husband, but she remains a supplicant. It does not seem, therefore, that the obligation to work necessarily strengthens rights.

There certainly is no guarantee that the value of the basic income will be maintained over the years, but this is also true of any other benefit or tax exemption. For example, under the UK State Earnings Related Pension Scheme, much criticized for its expense, the basic pension may well drop from 19% of average earnings in November 1985 to only 11% of average earnings in the year 2023[5]. The fact that most individuals and most households will stand to gain from basic income suggests there could be the electoral will to keep the level high. Indeed, it is just possible that the danger could not be underfunding, but Friedman's nightmare of the irresponsible masses voting the well-off minority to pay more and more and more! The past forty years in modern welfare states have seen both some benefits decline in value and others funded perhaps beyond a level the economy can sustain. There is little doubt both dangers would continue to exist with basic income.

These three objections to basic income as a means of preventing poverty argue that it would be ineffective in this aim. Other objectors argue that, effectiveness aside, the method basic income uses would be out of tune with the electorate's desires:

iv) People desire protection against loss of income, not against poverty, and so prefer earnings-related social insurance to any scheme offering only minimal security. Fair enough. Those who feel that way are fully able to insure themselves, either privately or through a trade union insurance scheme, against loss of earnings. The WRR report recommending a basic income for Holland positively encourages supplementary insurance, both state and voluntary.

v) In the USA, there is a strong antipathy to schemes that give money to millionaires who do not need it or to the feckless who do not deserve it. One can respond by reminding critics of the inefficiency of schemes that meet this popular requirement, and pointing out that some of America's most popular schemes do precisely what is supposed to be so unpopular: the popular social security system provides income for some who have private pensions and do not need social security: Rockefeller gets more tax-breaks than the luckiest welfare family gets cash, and all — including the Rockefellers — are entitled to free education (admittedly a benefit in kind, but with a substantial cash benefit in later life).

vi) A final, and intriguing, reservation about basic income comes from Philip Wogaman, Professor of Christian Social Ethics at Wesley Seminary, Washington DC[6]. To provide a basic income equally for all is to imply that those who currently lose out are the poor. In practice, the rich get many more breaks than the poor, so the poor should be compensated by a system such as negative income tax that is targeted specifically at them. I agree that, at first sight, basic income schemes give the image he criticizes, but in practice basic income can be as redistributive toward the poor as negative income tax, or even more so. It all depends on the actual levels and tax rates.

In conclusion, it seems to me that there is a viable argument for basic income as an effective way to prevent poverty. Even if the public and their politicians could be persuaded of this, however, it might not by itself be a good enough reason to gain sufficient support for basic income. In some countries, such as the UK, this is because few, even those on the lowest incomes, are willing to admit they are poor or in danger of becoming poor. In the USA, Hugh Heclo[7] has argued that ending poverty has never, even during the 1960s 'War on Poverty', been a goal that has appealed to the American people, though ending hunger, illiteracy and unnecessary ill-health have been. 'The main political problem with anti-poverty policy is that it is anti-poverty policy. The concept of income poverty is a statistical construction capable of interesting and animating economists and policy analysts but lacking a political reality capable of animating social action.' He concludes that the most effective measures against poverty are social security and tax measures in which most citizens feel there is something in it for them — which perhaps is not a bad description of basic income! But there are other considerations.

While basic income may be advocated as an efficient and practical reform of income-transfer arrangements, often people first get interested in it for rather more rarified reasons to do with ethics, morality, and ultimate values, before they later explore its practical operation. In the UK at present, several of the major churches are showing interest in basic income. In this chapter, I will explore two apparently contradictory ethics, a citizen ethic and a work ethic, both of which have led people to argue for basic income, and to suggest how they may be brought together[1].

Prosperity: Inheritance or reward?

In a chapter entitled 'Who Owns My Money?' in a previous book[2], I explored where human beings conceive the origin of their own prosperity to lie. Most wage and salary earners in a modern industrial society believe their own skills, training, effort and enterprise to be the source of their earnings which are therefore rightfully theirs to dispose of as they wish. Part of their earnings are *given* to other members of the household (to housewives and children); taxation is experienced as a *burden* or even as *theft*. Such language assumes that the only source and true claimant to my earnings are me myself.

Actually, this belief is slightly modified by many people today. Many breadwinners feel their family have a valid claim on their earnings, and some — often wives — feel that somehow their earnings do not actually belong to themselves but are the children's; so much so that some wives feel guilty about spending any part of their earnings on themselves. However, they still feel the source of their earnings to be their own labour, even if they themselves have little or no claim to the earnings.

Not all the human race feels or has felt like *homo industrialis*. In many peasant societies, the source of prosperity is believed to be the gods, or the ancestors, or the forest, and these are both implored and thanked for a good harvest. In the Christian tradition, there is the concept of stewardship in which personal talents are experienced not as belonging to myself but as gifts from God to be used responsibly in his service. Some of the more responsible aristocracy, of both today and yesteryear, consider their property to belong not to themselves as individuals but to the family line. I remember a neighbour, a member of the minor aristocracy, who, though in reduced circumstances, could not contemplate selling any of her possessions because they had all been inherited and she did not consider they belonged to her. For her, the fact that she lived in an England whose property law is based on individual possession altered her beliefs not a whit. And Senator Edward Kennedy, in a major speech in 1980, called for higher taxes for the rich based on a willingness to 'give back to our country in return for all it has given us.'

Even some industrialists have talked of stewardship as against ownership. Andrew Carnegie preached the need for captains of industry to see themselves as trustees rather than owners of the national wealth, and were morally bound to administer it for the general betterment. And Henry Lee Higginson, a leading member of the Boston business establishment, wrote in 1911: 'I do not believe that, because a man owns property, it belongs to him to do with as he pleases. The property belongs to the community, and he has charge of it, and can dispose of it, if it is well done and not with the sole regard to himself or to his stockholders.'[3]

Generally, though, the *nouveaux riches*, who have worked hard to raise themselves and their families out of poverty, are more likely to thank their labour than the gods for their prosperity. Their children and grandchildren, growing up in an environment not of poverty but of affluence, may see things differently; they know that affluence preceded their own efforts, indeed preceded their own existence. They may reject the possessive bourgeois individualism of their parents and join the ecology movement or a hippy commune in which it is taken for granted that we are the fortunate inheritors of a bounteous earth more than the personal architects of a prosperous city. The deep emotional commitment to one or the other of these views is revealed in the mutual rejection between the hippy and his dad, or indeed by the quiet divergence between the breadwinner who knows everything is earned and his wife, mother of three, who knows that ultimately life is a gift.

Who is right? Is prosperity our inheritance, or our reward? Simple observation surely reveals it to be both. An enterprising farmer decides to plough two fields, and prospers over his lazy neighbour who ploughs only one. This is undoubtedly due to his effort and enterprise. But without the steel plough, they'd both be back in stone age poverty. His prosperity is due first to his inheritance of technology and culture, and then to the enterprise and effort he applies to that inheritance.

Or try another mental experiment. You are a barber in San Francisco. It may well be that through hard work you can increase your earnings from $20,000 to $30,000. But what if you were a barber with equal intelligence and drive, and indeed using very similar equipment, in Bangladesh? Would you not then be fortunate to earn $200? Membership of a prosperous society *and* effort within that society are what produce the standard of living of you or me[4].

Most of us experience the human condition in two apparently contradictory ways. We know that many things are scarce, that we will sink if we do not struggle and strive and work. At the same time, we know that some of the best things in life, such as the air, life itself, and the love of our parents have simply been given. In the Christian tradition, this is called unmerited, unworked for, grace, or more simply, a blessing. In the national mythology of the USA, there is both the theme of unmerited plenty (the image of America as the promised land, provided freely by nature/destiny/God), and the theme of riches hard won in the struggle against natural scarcity (citizens trace themselves back to an ancestor who arrived off the boat with barely a suitcase and who proceeded to pull himself up by his own boot-straps). However, unlike peasant societies and aristocratic families, most of us in the west today in everyday speech forget to talk about human activity as a response to blessing and inheritance, but we have developed, I would claim overdeveloped, the language of human activity as the effort to overcome natural scarcity[5]. This is in addition to the understandable human propensity to congratulate oneself for one own prosperity, and to blame others ('society', 'environment', 'capitalism', 'socialism', or 'God') for any lack of prosperity.

It seems to me that a valid ethical justification for basic income, indeed for any method of distributing or redistributing the prosperity of a society, must take account of the following:

i) That my prosperity derives in part from my being born into and participating in a prosperous society. It is a gift, a blessing, an inheritance.

ii) That my prosperity derives in part from my own effort, talent and skill. It is the just reward for toil.

In addition, if basic income is to be politically acceptable in a modern society, it must also take into account:

iii) That those who are comfortably off or at least getting by, and indeed many who are not, like to focus on effort (ii) and do not like to be reminded too much of inheritance(i).

In other words, a justification for basic income that stresses inheritance over effort will be laughed at by most people, but a justification that ignores or is incompatible with inheritance will be ethically suspect and out of touch with reality.

Let's explore what such a justification might look like. It would draw on both the 'social dividend' tradition which stresses inheritance and the 'basic income' tradition which stresses effort.

Citizenship

Those who think of basic income as a social dividend (instead of or in addition to basic income as a technical device for preventing poverty) point out that since prosperity derives from participating in a technologically advanced society as well as from individual effort, income should be distributed not only through earnings but also through a 'social dividend'. The UK, or Germany, or the USA, could be compared to a highly capitalized firm, in which all citizens have shares; the firm should therefore pay out dividends to its citizens as well as wages to its paid workers. This line of thinking is found in Major Douglas, who stressed the productivity of the citizenry as the true security that underlies the creation of credit; in Oskar Lange who considered that nationalized industries should pay out dividends to citizens; in social dividend advocates such as Marie-Louise Duboin[6]; and with an echo in contemporary thinking about worker ownership, and in some of the more philosophical books of Bill Jordan.

The *state* has no rights to this dividend — we are certainly not talking here about a justification for higher taxation. It is *citizens* who have a right to the dividend, with government simply the most efficient channel through which the dividend may be paid. Those who have difficulty separating in their minds public spending from transfer payments between citizens arranged by government, often misunderstand social dividend at this point. They suppose the argument to be that, because prosperity derives from society as well as from individuals, therefore individuals should pay a tax to the state. That could perhaps be argued, but it has nothing to do with social dividend.

The Christian tradition, more than modern economics or

today's popular political rhetoric, has long understood that we respond to a generous inheritance rather than create wealth *ex nihilo*. As co-creators with God, our creative activity is essentially a response to receiving a gift rather than a pulling ourselves up from nothing by our own bootstraps. Some Christians have therefore been attracted by a social dividend which expresses this idea of wealth-creation as a response to gift. They suggest that to base economics or welfare on the illusion that the individual's own efforts are the sole source of his or her prosperity is a mark of human pride and vanity. This is illustrated in a recent booklet by Malcolm Torry[7]; 'Only by breaking the firm link between work and income shall we be able to enter into a covenant-relationship with the created order, and to understand it as a gift to be cherished and as the means whereby God gives wealth. Our present system persuades us that wealth is the product of our own effort and intelligence, and that those who do not work are paupers to be means-tested and given as little of the workers' wealth as possible. Only when we share a common source of income shall we understand that wealth belongs to us all as a gift of God, and that work of *all* kinds is an answer to God's invitation to take responsibility for his world.'

This quote hints at a further reason why some Christians, along with others, have become interested in basic income: it expresses the hope of fraternity, of togetherness as a people.

Need plus initiative

Those who conceive basic income more as a pragmatic and effective way to prevent poverty talk of human effort and enterprise as generators of wealth.

Any civilized modern society wants to protect its citizens from destitution, but dare not make protection so attractive that citizens decide to become poor; this was why the Victorian poor house was made so miserable. Nowadays we are more humane, and poor relief is less punitive, so now many more apply for and receive these benefits. In the UK, 14 million out of a population of 55 million receive income-tested benefits and thus also a disincentive to save or increase their earnings. In order to avoid abuse, most cash benefits for the able-bodied working age adult still require him or her to take or look for paid employment, but in practice this is leading to widespread cynicism in areas where there is no paid employment available. The consequences then of modern social security and welfare can be counter-productive. a) Income-tested benefits induce people to neither earn nor save, so they can qualify for benefits. b) Work tests induce dishonesty and cynicism. The desire to take paid employment and declare it for income tax is weakened.

Solution? Abolish income-testing and work tests! If the work ethic and personal initiative and integrity are to replace creeping dependency, then we must devise a policy that guarantees security against poverty without undermining the ability of the poor to better themselves or imposing work tests and thus inducing cynicism. This indeed has been the main ground on which I argue for basic income. It is a civilized way of avoiding what Hermione Parker calls 'the moral hazard' of selective, income-tested welfare benefits[8]. The two ethical principles behind this approach are: a) identifying and meeting financial need, b) providing a framework in which personal responsibility, freedom, and enterprise can flourish among the poor as well as among the better off.

It seems to me that this argument complements our argument about inheritance and citizenship. Together, they imply that prosperity depends both on membership of a prosperous economy and on personal effort. However, while the citizenship argument may appeal to theologians and some social philosphers and is certainly worth propagating more widely, it will strike dissonant chords in the moral repertoire of many taxpayers and voters. Those who advocate basic income would be wise to rely mainly on the argument that basic income will restore the financial security, personal integrity and willingness to work that current welfare arrangements are eroding among an increasing number of people in the modern welfare state.

Objections

In these two approaches, I have in fact appealed to altogether four arguments. The 'social dividend' approach appeals to both the idea of gift, and the idea of economic co-operation on a collectively inherited property. The 'basic income' approach appeals to both an argument about basic needs and an argument about liberty. None of these four arguments are without their problems, which have been summarized by Robert van der Veen[9]:

Gift. The notion of our economic inheritance as a gift captures the sense in which basic income, and what it represents, is not conditional on our personal talent or effort. Some, however, argue that basic income should be a right, and gifts and blessings are not convincing foundations of a right. You can count your blessings, but not count on them.

Collective property. This approach argues that personal effort is productive only in so far as I co-operate with others to use the economy and the technology that we have inherited from the labours of previous generations. Earnings represent personal effort, basic income the fruits of co-operation.

This argument might be rejected by descendants of the classic Lockean defense of private property: in the past, unequally endowed individuals created differing fortunes for themselves, and felt they had the right to pass these on to their own biological heirs. To say that their unequal efforts now represent a *common* heritage is to elevate equality of outcome above the rights of private property. Our argument therefore is at root egalitarian, and this egalitarianism needs justifying if it is to be persuasive.

Furthermore, why should income deriving from jointly using collective assets be distributed to able-bodied persons who refuse to participate in the current labour process? While the notion of a collective inheritance may serve as a foundation for a general right to non-labour income, it could also be taken to imply that this right incurs a general duty to work. Some advocates of basic income, such as Gorz and Alder-Karlsson, suggest precisely this[10]. Thus the collective property/economic co-operation approach does not by itself provide an ethical basis for *unconditional* basic income.

Basic needs. This argument presumes that each citizen has a right to have their basic needs met, and basic income is the most efficient way to meet these needs. But different individuals have differing needs, so one might argue that a more discriminating method could be more appropriate. If one level, or a very few levels, of basic income are all that can be allowed, how can basic income be pitched so as to meet the very varied needs that individuals have? (I explored the problems here in Chapter Four.) Unless basic income can be pitched high enough to meet everyone's financial needs, which it cannot, surely we should retain the welfare state principle of giving priority to satisfying the needs of the under-endowed and disadvantaged (the needs of the needy)? With inadequate funds for a full basic income, almost everyone's conception of justice would lead them to support the welfare state principle of reserving help for those who demonstrably either need it or have paid for it. In fact, the basic income proposals of Parker, the MacDonald Commission and the Dutch WRR report concur with this. They propose a mixture of basic income plus extra help to those who need it or (in the WRR report) to those who have insured themselves.

Liberty. The argument that basic income could foster initiative and enterprise rests not only on the premise that this is necessary for a healthy and affluent economy but also on the premise that personal liberty should have a high priority. (This I explore more fully in Section v of this chapter.) Basic income gives everyone the option of free time with which to pursue their personal projects. But what of those who are by nature industrious and/or have expensive needs and who therefore choose to work long and hard? They certainly have the liberty to do this, but why should they lose in taxes some of the fruits of their personal project, while those who decide to pursue other, unpaid projects reap the full benefit of their project? It is not easy to argue why society should offer equal free time to all but tax the freedom to get rich by hard work and smartness.

Welfare and wealth

There is another ethical argument for basic income, which is also backed up by the evidence of economic history, over against the materialist ethics espoused by many politicians and economists.

Their dominant view holds that a nation can afford welfare only when it has accumulated the wealth to pay for it. Wealth creation is the main aim of modern governments, with welfare a mere by-product of wealth.

This materialist philosophy was scathingly attacked by the Old Testament prophets who could clearly see in the countries surrounding Ancient Israel that their materialism certainly did not lead to fairness or well-being, nor even guarantee material prosperity. When amassing wealth becomes either a personal or a national aim, then at what point does care for the unfortunate and the needy magically emerge? All too often, it never does. Moreover, when greed rules, material prosperity itself may well suffer.

Instead the prophets called the Israelite people to a different set of values: to deal justly and to care for their neighbour. This can have interesting consequences. When people deal fairly with one another, mutual trust develops, and a climate is created in which business can flourish. When justice is the aim, prosperity may be the result! But paradoxically, when prosperity becomes the *aim*, it may begin to slip from our hands. Economic historians have argued that it was precisely this Biblical ethical framework, rather than the profit motive, which gave the original impetus to modern capitalism in Western Europe. But as soon as the profit motive becomes dominant and other values wither, then decay sets into the relationships that undergird a previously prosperous economy.

Basic income is attractive to many in the Judaic-Christian tradition because it restores this principle that nations are called to pursue not prosperity but justice for the weak. Welfare or *shalom* — a structure of fairness and compassion — is the only basis for a truly stable and prosperous society. How this might work with basic income, in particular how it could free and unblock the labour market, should become apparent later in this chapter.

Basic income crops up frequently in discussions about the long-term direction of industrial society; indeed, this is a major way in which people first hear about basic income and develop an interest. It seems to me that the importance of such discussions about the role of basic income in some future society is not that we will somehow be able to afford basic income in the future: I have already argued that this hope is beside the point: governments notoriously find money for what they wish. No, the value of the futures debate is that it reveals that any long-term government policy must be not only appropriate for our present values, traditions and economy, but also flexible enough to cope with possible future circumstances. We cannot predict the future, but we must think about what might happen. In particular, we must devise tax and social security policies that can cope with mass unemployment and widespread automation as well as full employment. At the very least, policies must reflect *current* values and circumstances, which tax and social security in the UK certainly do not do at present.

Despite a historically high proportion of the population in paid employment today, future scenarios are often preoccupied with the effect of automation on the demand for paid labour. What if automation should create productivity so high that just a few workers can create the goods and services for an affluent society? Should steps be taken to share out the paid work? If not, how will money or goods be distributed to those without paid work? If previous chapters have explored basic income assuming a business-as-usual economy, how might basic income be appropriate to unstaffed automation? Would it be more appropriate than the tax and welfare arrangements we currently have?[1]

Two sectors

In this scenario, there will be two main classes. There is the new working class composed largely of an elite of highly paid technicians each controlling phenomenally expensive and productive equipment. Then there is the mass, the new leisured class, funded by welfare benefits, perhaps some kind of basic income or, worse, the charity food banks currently sprouting up all over North America. This is James Robertson's Hyper-Expansionist (HE) scenario[2].

The condition of the 'leisure' class is cause for concern. On welfare benefits alone, people's existence could hardly be termed leisure, and even in a society so affluent as to afford generous benefits, leisure would involve mainly a freedom to buy and consume, not a freedom to lead an active and independent life. Charles Handy envisages 'an army of dependent layabouts living on their social wage, desperate for the modern variety of bread and circuses, growing obese in front of their television sets in human battery coops . . .'[3] The remarkably enduring desire for paid employment, revealed in survey after survey would add to the despondency of this non-working mass. Moreover, the leisured class would have lost the two major sources of political power: 'The condition of their existence would be dependent on those who generated the wealth, and it would be this "new working class" which would ultimately control the levers of power: the "leisure class", after all, would not have any significant control of capital, nor would they have the power to withdraw their labour.'[4] With little power to resist the value of basic income being pared away, they might not be exactly 'obese' in front of their televisions.

I have yet to meet an advocate of basic income who is not horrified by this scenario.

To date, there is evidence of another kind of dual-sector economy emerging, most notably in the USA, which has to some extent succeeded in replacing the leisured/unemployed class with a class of low-wage workers often enjoying neither good conditions of work nor job security. These may work in service industries such as cleaning, restaurants and laundries, picking up the crumbs from the overladen table of the other class of affluent workers. Or they may form the periphery of large businesses. Employers increasingly value the flexibility provided by a dual workforce — a core of trained, skilled workers whom they cannot afford to lose and who therefore are given high wages and good terms, and a periphery of unskilled, poorly paid workers who can be laid off or taken on whenever trading circumstances demand.

This pattern is taking two slightly different forms. Trans-national corporations often employ a workforce in the Third World, leaving few low-paid jobs for countries such as Britain or Belgium which consequently suffer high unemployment. In the USA, however, the Third World is arriving across the Rio Grande every day, willing to take on such jobs within the USA itself. But even in Britain, the dual-sector economy exists, notably with part-time non-unionized women in the peripheral sector, with only limited protection by employment legislation and the first to be laid off in recession.

How does basic income relate to this dual labour market? One view described in detail in Chapter 6 v, and advocated by the Dutch WRR report, is that basic income will lead to a proliferation of low-paying, perhaps part-time, jobs (some even done from home) that currently do not exist. Though this will extend the dual labour market, basic income will provide peripheral workers with a security, a financial base and choices that they currently do not enjoy.

If this view sees basic income as a *cause* of the extension of the dual-labour market, another view sees it as a necessary financial *compensation* for a dual labour market which is expanding anyway, whether we like it or not. Basic income provides a measure of security and indeed bargaining power for those who otherwise would have none.

A third view is that basic income must be linked with a national minimum wage and tighter employment legislation in order to protect conditions for the low-paid[5].

Two times

If the previous scenario envisages a society divided into those with (good) work and those with little or no work, another scenario envisages the work being shared around so that we all have the opportunity to work at some time during our lives. Our lives will be divided into those periods when we engage in paid work, and those periods when we do other things. To some extent this is already happening, with entry into the world of paid employment delayed through higher education or youth unemployment, and with increasing numbers of men pre-maturely ending their period of paid employment in their fifties as redundancy merges into retirement.

Some writers of a left/ecological bent look forward to a society in which there is a rich mixture of paid and unpaid activity, with the paid activity available to all for at least some part of their life. This vision may have a more socialist aspect, as in André Gorz, or a more ecological, small-scale, decentralized emphasis, as in Robertson's Sane, Humane, Ecological (SHE) alternative. Both writers envisage basic income as a key part of such a society[6]. Their hope and their belief is well-stated by Erich Fromm in a classic early article on 'The Psychological Aspects of the Guaranteed Income'[7]: 'Only with the transformation of *homo consumens* into a productive, active person will man experience freedom in true independence and not in unlimited choice of commodities.'

Bill Jordan has a similar vision of the good society. He points out[8] that if there is not enough paid work, there are three ways of sharing it around. One is to reduce the length of the working week or the working life. It is difficult to reduce the working week voluntarily because it reduces take-home pay. Work-sharing, hailed in theory as a good thing, is routinely resisted in practice for just this reason, especially — and understandably — by low-paid workers who cannot afford to earn less. Basic income schemes help low-paid workers' households, and this might provide a certain leeway that could enable low-paid workers to be more enthusiastic about work-sharing. Reducing the duration of the working life, along with job sharing, raises a similar problem: reduced pension rights. Basic income would certainly help here, because the basic income for the elderly, unlike current pensions, is not dependent on number of years of full contributions.

The second option is to increase the direction of labour by the state. Jordan rejects this, not just because of its inefficiency but more importantly because it is a denial of the key value of autonomy, the ability of individuals to make their own decisions and plans. Most Western Europeans and North Americans would, I think, share his feeling at this point, though Americans are enthusiastic about something very similar, namely workfare which requires welfare recipients to work for their benefits, and this is now being debated in the federal legislature.

The third option, which may sound strange to some but clearly makes sense in a society in which automation has reduced employers' demand for labour, is to allow the right not to earn. If the right to earn is an invention of an industrial society that needed wage labour, a post-industrial society that needs to shed labour might reasonably offer in addition the right not to earn. This leaves it up to the individual citizen whether s/he wishes to earn money and for how long during the day, week, year, or lifetime. I have argued elsewhere[9] that if today 10% of the workforce is involuntarily unemployed, and perhaps another 10% is employed but could think of better things to do were they financially able, then giving them the right not to be in paid employment might very well help release paid jobs that would make the right to earn a reality for the other 10%. Basic income would go some way toward giving everyone the right not to earn which may be essential if the right to earn is to have any substance in a society that shuns the direction of labour (whether of a left-wing variety, or a right-wing variety that advocates workfare or directs female labour back into the home). The Jordan/Walter vision of the good society is of people having the choice to move in and out of paid employment, or if you like in and out of sabbaticals; a society of willing employees, with productive periods out of employment to pursue personal or household projects of one's own choosing (childrearing, charitable work, education, etc, etc.)[10]. Other writers, such as Edward Bellamy, André Gorz, and Gunnar Adler-Karlsson, argue that basic income should be available only after one has done 'national service' in the labour market for a certain number of years, but otherwise their vision of freely chosen productive labour is similar.

This option to move out of paid employment is sorely needed in Britain at the moment. We have one of the highest levels of unemployment in Europe, but also one of the highest proportions of people in paid employment. One can only conclude that one reason for the high unemployment is the unusually high proportion of the population in the market for jobs. How then to reduce the workforce? The usual answers, such as raising the school leaving age, reducing the retirement age, and suggesting married women should not take paid work, all smack of paternalism, bureaucracy and authoritarianism; not all children wish to stay on at school, not all older workers want to retire, and certainly not all wives want to stay at home! By contrast, basic income gives individuals *themselves* more choice when to be in the workforce, or at least more choice as to the number of hours a week they work. In particular, it could give full-time employees the choice to go part-time.

Many critics detest both the dual-labour market and shared employment. They agree that even with automation there is plenty of work to do, but they would rather that as much of it as possible were paid. Many women in the labour movement are all too familiar with the work of caring being dumped on them by either husbands or right-wing governments returning the care once provided by salaried employees in the health service to unpaid female members of the private household. What has happened in the UK over the past few years is less paid employment for women in the national health service, and more unpaid work for them at home looking after relatives discharged from psychiatric or geriatric hospital in the name of 'community care'. They certainly do not look forward to a 'SHE' future in which they still do the dirty work of caring, unpaid.

If basic income is compatible with a reduced period of earning per lifetime, I have also argued it is compatible with full employment. Political goals come and go: basic income provides a platform upon which several political goals can be pursued. It could provide a tax/welfare structure that can endure through changing governments and employment policies. Given that we do not know which way as a society we shall go, or want to go, it is surely important to have something stable like basic income that could enable the two-sector economy to move into full employment or into the two-time economy.

The arguments so far have been put forward by people of all political persuasions and of none. In the next three sections, I look at three specifically ideological arguments for basic income: that it is a prerequisite for a free labour market, in turn a prerequisite for political freedom; that it is the key to pursuing socialism; and that by providing economic independence for all, it provides a key to the liberation of women. In each section, I will not be concerned primarily with whether a free market, socialism, or independence for women, are valid goals but whether basic income is likely to help achieve these goals. Readers will doubtless have their own commitments to certain goals, and abhorrence of other goals. My purpose is to enable readers to see whether, given their commitments, basic income is something they should take seriously.

The free market

The free market philosophy is both economic and political, its chief aim being to maximize personal liberty. It claims that free markets are not only the most efficient and productive way to organize the economy known to humankind, but also a prerequisite for political freedom[1]. When markets are not free, production and distribution are inefficient and citizens become all too aware that they are not getting what they want; state control is then necessary to stamp out dissent. In particular, if I am not free to leave one employer for another, then my freedom of speech and indeed my whole life can be controlled by my employer — which in communist societies is generally the state.

Although western democracies have a free, or nearly free, market for many goods and services, none have a free market for labour. According to free market theory, there are three major reasons for this. One is trade unions, which restrict the freedom of both employer and employee to bargain freely with each other as individuals. The second limit on the market for labour is taxation, which now is levied on virtually all full-time employees and some part-time ones too. This means in effect that employer and employee cannot freely negotiate a wage, because government steps in and removes some of it.

Thirdly, and crucially for market advocates of basic income, there is a floor for wages, at least for heads of households. Being civilized, modern western societies guarantee that families will not starve; but this means that breadwinners have little incentive to work for less than welfare payments. Of the many goods and services for which there is a demand at a given price, some can be produced only by paying workers less than the subsistence/welfare level. The result is these tasks are not performed. Or the work is done for free within the home, or by workers in the Third World who will accept much lower wages. The result is unemployment in the West.

Wives of employed husbands in most western countries are often not subject to these three restrictions: they are rarely entitled to welfare benefits, are rarely taxed on part-time earnings, and are often not unionized. It is not surprising, then, that more and more employment has become available for them, at the cost of full-time, male, unionized jobs. The United States, too, has been exempt to some extent from these limitations on the labour market: the union movement is much weaker than in European countries, income tax is lower, and welfare benefits for men are inadequate once their unemployment benefit has run out.

The result of all this, according to free market theory, is unemployment — especially for unskilled men in certain European countries. This is economically inefficient, entailing lost production and extra taxes on workers to pay for other people's unemployment benefit; personally enervating for those suffering unemployment; and politically dangerous, because large masses of dissatisfied unemployed workers have to be controlled, which leads to new powers being taken by police and state, which in turn erodes the basic liberty of the people (there is evidence this is already happening in the UK).

What to do? Free marketeers are usually agreed on reducing union power and reducing taxes; they are less agreed about what to do about the floor on wages, which some see as *the* major cause of unemployment. There seem to be four options consistent with free market theory.

The first is to follow Charles Murray's logic and abolish the minimum wage, abolish all publicly funded benefits for chief breadwinners, and leave them to the mercies of private charities. This indeed is already happening to some extent in the United States. Many new low-paying jobs will be created, which these desperate men will have to take in order to survive. However, apart from any concern about the harshness of such a policy, it also does not seem very effective in attaining its own self-proclaimed goal — personal liberty. What freedom, what autonomy to pursue personally chosen plans and projects, is there if you have to toil every waking hour at one dollar an hour? One only has to read Dickens to know such a person has little personal liberty[2].

A second, and more modest, proposal that is seriously discussed on the right in Britain is to reduce rather than abolish benefits, to lower the floor rather than demolish it. This would create a substantial number of low-paid jobs, which it would be rational for the unemployed to take and they would regain the dignity of supporting their own families[3]. Again, however, apart from being unacceptable in many quarters, this proposal could succeed only partially in attaining its own goals. It still raises the Dickensian nightmare of slavery to ill-paying, bad jobs. Moreover, by retaining a floor to earnings, it still leaves the labour market unfree; it's just a little less unfree, because the floor is a little lower. With increasing affluence and automation over the coming years, what is to prevent political

pressure raising the floor again, which is of course precisely
what has happened since Victorian days.

A third option, proposed by free marketeer Milton
Friedman, is negative income tax[4] where the state tops up the
income of low income households. Friedman argues that the
relief of poverty is one of the few functions that government
should be involved in. Nobody likes to see beggars in the street,
and it is unfair to rely on private charity to clear the streets and
ease our feelings; we all benefit from the relief of poverty, so we
should all pay. The problem with present welfare arrangements, especially in the United States where they tend to
provide benefits in kind or benefits earmarked for food or health
care, is that they intrude into the privacy and liberty of the
poor. For those on welfare, the government has come to mean
'Big Brother'; they are told how much they may spend on food,
rent, and clothing; they have to get permission from an official
to rent a house or buy even second-hand furniture; mothers
may have their male visitors checked on at any hour of the day
or night. So, Friedman argues, get rid of all the red tape, get rid
of the maze of earmarked and in-kind benefits, and give the
poor the money. Let them spend it according to their own
values. Friedman has long advocated a negative income tax,
targeted at the poor, and removed as claimants better
themselves. Exceptional cases of additional need would be met
by private charity which Friedman believes more able than
public bureaucracies to respond to the particular needs of
particular persons. In Friedman's scheme, it would always be
worthwhile taking a paid job, however low the wage.

Friedman's argument has much to commend it, and has
influenced the thinking behind basic income. However, it bears
the costs of any negative income tax scheme, mentioned in
Chapter 2: stigma due to a continuing distinction between
taxpayers and claimants; disincentives to take paid work if the
negative tax payment is based on the wage without taking into
account the costs of getting to work; inducement to family
break-up because of the household, not the individual, being
the unit of assessment (a household can split, and gain two lots

of negative income tax). Crucially, it institutionalizes a high marginal tax rate on the working poor, precisely the people — according to free market theory — who most require an incentive to better themselves.

Basic income

The fourth option is to introduce basic income, arguably the only way to free the labour market without at the same time eroding the freedom of the poor. In the hypothetical case of every individual receiving a basic income sufficient for subsistence, wages can be fixed entirely by supply and demand without reference to subsistence or 'the family wage'[5]. By removing the subsistence element from wages, employers, employees and trade unions will be able to negotiate freely. Employers will be able to offer the market wage for any job they want done, and will be able to find people willing to work for that wage. If they cannot attract labour, then they are offering less than the market price and will have to offer more; if they are inundated with applications, they can reduce wages. Trade unions will retain an important role negotiating a fair market wage and providing employees with negotiating power equal to that of employers, but unions will no longer be haunted by the fear of unemployment or driven to ask for a wage sufficient to support a family.

Since the price of labour will have no minimum, employers will increase their demand for labour until the demand for jobs is satisfied. Unemployment, except frictional unemployment for those changing jobs, will be abolished. Not only will there be no unemployed people, but the very concept of unemployment will cease to have any meaning. The choice facing many people today, unemployment or full-time employment to support a family, will fade into a much expanded choice of how much household members wish to add to their basic incomes, and how many hours of work are required to earn that.

Not only hours worked in the week, but also hours worked in a lifetime, will become more flexible. At present, people are expected to enter the world of paid work when they leave school or college, often at an age fixed by law, and to leave that world at a statutory age of retirement. These fixed points of entry and departure are reinforced by changes in income — from parental allowance or college grant to wages, and from wages to pension. With a basic income from cradle to grave, people will be more able to choose when to start or leave the world of paid work rather than have to fit into a school leaving age, and to choose a retirement age that has to do with the individual's own life projects rather than the calculations of government actuaries.

Indeed, just as the concept of unemployment will become redundant, so official ages for retirement and for leaving high school could be abolished. At present, many a child masters the three 'R's by age ten or eleven, and then learns little else for the next few years in which it is forced by law to remain in school. Maybe not till later in adulthood does the person realize the value of education, but then cannot afford to take a sabbatical to go back to school. Learning is most effective when the learner is motivated, and our laws forcing children to be in school till age 16 or 18 are infringements on personal liberty that are not even effective in producing an educated citizenry. The opportunity to leave school on being able to demonstrate s/he can read, write and do sums, followed by the opportunity to return to school whenever s/he sees the need, would be a logical part of a basic income package: efficient, productive, and promoting personal liberty.

This would require a basic income tailored to the costs of living for various ages, so that each person (whether aged 14 or 74) could freely choose how much paid employment to take. It would probably imply a steadily increasing basic income from 60 or 65 onwards as old age brings extra needs and costs, but not one age at which basic income is suddenly more than doubled as in Parker's BIG 1(a) scheme (see my Table 1). Only then would elderly people have a free choice when to cease or scale down their paid work.

A final advantage is that it will become easier to modernize industry. At present, this is often resisted by workforces who, correctly, fear being made redundant. With basic income, unemployment would not be so dire a threat to income and liberty as it currently is in the West, and workers would be less concerned to preserve outmoded jobs.

So, according to this free market scenario of life under basic income, not only would wage levels be freed from current restraints, but so would hours of work, dates of entry and departure from the labour market, and plant modernization. All this, of course, would be possible only if basic income were sufficient to meet basic living costs, which I have argued is not feasible except for those excluded from the labour market by age or disability. We are therefore in reality talking about a basic income, topped up by earnings, family help, or residual income-tested state assistance. The liberties described in the previous few pages could not fully materialize, but the overall effect could well be to enhance substantially these liberties.

When the theory of free markets was first enunciated by Adam Smith at the end of the eighteenth century, there were indeed few restraints on the determination of wage levels. The major restraints of trade unionism, income tax, and the floor created by welfare payments have all arisen since then. Free marketeers have to accept basic income if they are to realize their eighteenth century dream without reverting to eighteenth century economic insecurity.

To accept basic income, however, free marketeers will have to let one part of their thinking be turned upside down. It is widely assumed that a society can only afford welfare payments, including proposals such as basic income, if the market is freed and allowed to flourish. But there is another side to this coin: the market can be freed to flourish only when there is well-being, and basic income supplies that. It may be that wealth creation is necessary for welfare provision, but it may also be that welfare provision in the form of basic income is necessary for wealth creation. We may yet have to relearn the message of the Old Testament prophets that *shalom* — well-being, seeking justice for the poor, living in peace with one another — is the basis on which material prosperity is built; it is not an optional extra available only once a society has created material wealth.

Market objections to basic income

Leaving aside still the many objections to free market theory, what reservations are free marketeers themselves likely to have about the argument that basic income is necessary to free the market?

I think the most likely objection is that basic income would involve a huge increase in government interference in the economy and in people's lives, and is therefore a threat to freedom. This objection I think is mistaken. As for government interference in the economy, basic income would be far less interfering than the current maze of incentives and subsidies, from tax relief on mortgage interest to subsidies for new small firms, that it would replace. As for interference in people's lives, there could be somewhat less interference for most taxpayers who would benefit from a tax credit rather than tax allowances. In that tax allowances and reliefs would be reduced or abolished, it would be much easier for taxpayers to plan their finances, and many would be able to say goodbye to their accountants. For many children and wives, there would be the new 'interference' of a regular basic income cheque, but there is no evidence that mothers in the UK who receive weekly child benefit payments experience this as an interference in their lives! And for those currently on welfare benefits, there would be a massive reduction in interference, as described by Milton Friedman. On this point far Right and far Left agree that the authorities should stop hassling the poor[7].

Secondly, free marketeers may well point to the high tax

rates that would be necessary to sustain basic income. In the USA, taxation would have to increase. In European countries, though it need not increase overall taxation (see Chapter Four), basic income would make any major reduction unlikely. I have discussed some of the possible economic effects of this in Chapter Five, but free marketeers are ultimately concerned that *any* income tax impinges on personal liberty to do as one pleases with one's own money. The choices for free marketeers are: 1) Continuing as at present, with high marginal tax rates for the poor and major infringements on their liberty. 2) The Murray/Minford option: this reduces marginal tax rates for the poor, but still denies them major liberties. 3) Negative income tax: this is an improvement for the poor both in terms of marginal tax and in terms of liberty. 4) Basic income: depending on the marginal tax rate, this puts the poor on rather more equal terms with the rest of society in terms of liberty, but at the cost of somewhat higher taxes for the better off.

A third objection might note that the guarantor of freedom is small property. Large property, owned by an individual or a company, typically coerces other people, and the effective remedy is not further concentration of this property in the hands of government, but its dispersal to the citizenry. There is a key difference between large property and small property, 'for small property is essentially defensive, an embodiment of freedom from something or somebody; while large property always run the risk of being invasive and grasping, embodying therefore freedom to do something to somebody.'[8] In this view, the resources going into basic income would be better used to enable every citizen to become a property owner; in this view, which I do not hold, tax relief on mortgage interest and on pension premiums (themselves a form of property) are precisely what we need!

Such a property-owning democracy could indeed enhance freedom for some employed householders, though it is difficult to see how owning a few shares in a huge transnational corporation gives the kind of freedom provided by owning your own house, land or small business. Moreover, questions have to be asked about the wives and children who typically do not hold the title deeds of their home, nor have pensions in their own right, nor own shares; they would perhaps have more independence and liberty with a personal basic income than as dependents of the title-holder in the household. And there is a question about those who in the transitional period to this property-owning democracy remain without property; would their independence and liberty not be enhanced by personal basic incomes? Small property may be a guarantor of freedom but, outside of a peasant society in which property means land on which one may subsist, it may not be a guarantor against poverty. Shares and mortgages don't feed the kids.

Non-market objections

The free market argument for basic income faces some objections that, though not based on free market assumptions, are often voiced by those who are fellow travellers with free marketeers[9].

The first objection disagrees with the basic analysis. It claims that unemployment is not caused by wages so high they price citizens out of jobs, but by wages so low that firms need not invest in modern machinery; productivity declines, and we are forced into competition with low-wage Third World countries on terms we can never win. Right-wing British MP Ralph Howell's solution[10] is to impose a national minimum wage and for the state to offer work at that wage to any who cannot find employment. Welfare payments to the idle able-bodied are ended. This will keep wages up, induce firms to modernize, and provide labour to tidy up the environmental and other sores of an ageing industrial landscape. This kind of workfare programme, where recipients have to work for their benefits, is currently popular in the USA. The analysis of too low, not too high, wages seems reasonable to a simple-minded non-economist like myself. What seems certain about workfare solutions, whether of the Howell variety or the American variety, is that they carry a price in liberty.

Often associated with workfare is a moral objection to the free market argument for basic income. This is that paid employment is a responsibility of citizenship and morally uplifting for people; they should not have the choice not to work. Certainly this feeling is very strong among ordinary people in North America, Britain, Scandinavia, and other European countries outside perhaps Southern Ireland and the Latin countries. I have already argued at some length that a basic income that gives people the right not to work could actually make work more of a reality than it currently is for millions of people, but this may cut little ice with those who believe on moral grounds that able-bodied men should not have the right to opt out of paid employment.

I do wonder, though, how many people actually do believe this on *moral* grounds? If they did, then they surely would be up in arms about tax exemptions that enable the rich not to work, or minimal capital transfer taxes that enable the children of the rich not to work. I respect Andrew Carnegie who never retired and said he'd not leave his children a cent lest they escape from the moral virtue of labour, but I do not really believe those who claim idleness to be a sin yet long to be millionaires so that they can one day indulge in just that sin. I fear that the so-called moral virtue of labour is appealed to mainly as a rationalization by those who have to work, or as a stick with which to beat the poor.

But let us for a moment take at face value the belief in the moral virtue of paid employment. It contradicts the belief in personal liberty. All societies have contradictions in their core values,[11] and it seems to me that this particular contradiction is central to western democracies. In the USA, I meet traditionalists who are insistent that husbands should be out working and wives at home making apple pie, yet who would go to war to defend personal liberty. In the UK, I know feminists who made *choice* the rallying cry of the 1970s, yet profoundly believe in the merits of paid labour and resist basic income because they are appalled at the prospect of women choosing to go home to make apple pie. It is these contradictory values within the same person that makes it impossible to predict how individuals will respond to basic income. But I hazard a generalization. Those, even 'modern' feminists, whose traditional belief in the merit of paid labour wins out tend to reject basic income; those, even hard-nosed economists, whose passion for personal liberty wins out tend to be at least willing to consider basic income.

If there is an argument that places basic income at the centre of a free market philosophy, there are also arguments that make it the key to socialism[1].

According to classic Marxism, a basic cause of inequality and exploitation within capitalism is that the capitalist can make his property work for him, while the propertyless worker has nothing but his labour power to sell if he is to keep body and soul together. While in a so-called free market the capitalist employer is free, his workers are very far from free, especially where employers take active steps to make their workers dependent on the firm by monopolizing housing (as often in Victorian Britain) or leisure facilities (as in Japan) which are then offered as perks of the job.

Marx therefore argued that property — the means of production — must be returned collectively to the workers. This demands a socialist revolution in which the state takes over the means of production. It should then be possible to move from this state socialism to Marx's vision of communism, based on the principle 'From each according to his abilities, to each according to his needs'.

Marx's vision has yet to materialize in any advanced industrial economy. In Western Europe and North America, the workers have been bought off with higher wages and house ownership, and union power eroded either by deliberate government legislation or by gradual replacement of the large factory by the white collar office with its quiescent middle class workforce. Those countries which have undergone a Soviet style revolution or take-over have not progressed beyond the phase in which the state controls the means of production; they have yet to arrive at true communism and hope has almost entirely waned that they ever will. In western democracies, nationalized industries have followed a similar pattern, with profits (or losses) accruing to the state rather than to the workers or to the citizenry at large on the basis of need.

The crisis for the left in the West, therefore, is that the classic Marxist route to communism now seems likely neither to happen nor to succeed. How else may modern capitalist societies progress to communism?

The intriguing consequence of basic income is that it would put the worker in the same position as the capitalist: it gives him or her independent means. S/he will not depend entirely on the employer for survival, and the most unacceptable aspect of exploitation will be removed. Workers will have more power. Individually, they will have more ability to quit a bad job, and employers may find they will have to offer better wages or better conditions in order to attract workers to inherently unpleasant jobs. Collectively, trade unions will be in a better bargaining position. Some low paid workers might even threaten to leave en masse, permanently, knowing that life on basic income is nothing like current life on the dole; this ultimate threat is there in the background, in addition to the strike weapon.

Basic income provides not just the right to refuse work, but the possibility of using that right (which is more powerful than the right to strike) to ask questions about and negotiate to improve the value of both the product and the process of work. As a radical document from a UK Claimants' Union put it:[2] 'Instead of work being accepted unquestioningly as everyone's lot, people would think before getting involved in any communal project. When the equation work equals money equals necessities is broken people will be free to ask Work equals what? For whom? Why? Is the product necessary and to whom? Is it maybe shoddy or even actually harmful? Is the work pleasant to do, can it be made such, if not, could it be automated? Is the work being hampered by its bureaucratic management, with only a few people controlling the information and the pathways to getting things done? Is the work being arranged in the most efficient way?'

Under basic income, not only will employers in a free labour market be able to offer high wages to attract skilled labour but also workers will be able to demand higher wages for unpleasant work. Poorly paid, non-union, female labour will have as effective a right as older unions to say 'no' to bad work. High wages will no longer reflect the power of particular unions or professional associations but the necessity, skill or unpleasantness of the job.

Socialists disagree with the free market analysis described in the previous section, for even with the removal of all restraints the labour market does not provide freedom for the labourer. There is a 'fundamental difference between the labour market and a commodity market. A supplier on a commodity market can simply withdraw his product and stop producing it if he is unable to sell it for a profitable price. That is why there is rarely a persistent excess supply on commodity markets, apart from overproduction for political reasons such as the oil market or the European dairy market. For a supplier on the labour market, that is an employee, however, there is no free choice. His whole subsistence, and often that of his wife and children too, depends on the one commodity he 'produces'; his labour. So he must accept whatever wage rate is offered him on the labour market. As a consequence, labour supply (especially of adult males) is highly inflexible, hardly reacting to changes in the wage rate. The introduction of a basic income would (to some extent) eliminate the dependence of the worker on his labour and enable him to act as a free negotiator on the labour market.'[3] We see here a hint of how, curiously, socialist and free market arguments for basic income begin to coincide. Basic income not only frees the labour market in a way that delights free marketeers, it also gives a freedom to the worker (either individually or collectively) that is the very hallmark of Marx's vision of communism!

At present the labour market is organized on the principle 'From each according to his need, to each according to his ability'. People work because they need to, and they are rewarded largely according to their ability and what the market is prepared to pay for that ability. Robert van der Veen and

Philippe Van Parijs, in their provocative essay 'A Capitalist Road to Communism',[4] suggest that basic income could enable this goal to be realized without the state first having to own the means of production. With basic income, people work because they have skills and abilities for which the market is prepared to pay (from each according to their ability); and their basic needs are automatically met independently of their labour contribution (to each according to his need). Collective ownership of the means of production is not only not likely in present conditions in the West, it is also not necessary for the attainment of justice! Basic income unblocks the log-jam in which western socialists have found themselves.

How might all this come about? Van der Veen and Van Parijs argue that the crisis of welfare together with the perverse effects of all the other options will lead advanced industrial economies to implement basic income. Rapid automation together with limits to the expansion of paid employment will turn the adoption of basic income and the shift to an egalitarian society from a utopian dream to a historical necessity, not in the sense that it will happen automatically but in the sense that, given the material conditions, human reason will eventually generate the political forces to bring it about.

Objections from trade unionists

By far the most common so-called socialist objections to basic income come not on theoretical grounds but from practical trade unionists. Many unionists object that it begins to decouple income from labour. They do not like the idea of the average household receiving part of its income from the basic income of non-earning members. I think there are several worries that many unionists have about this.

Firstly, they fear that the role and power of trade unions will be eroded. Trade unions have long seen their raison d'être as the maintenance of the living standards of the working class through collective action to maximize wages. If living standards are maintained in part by the basic incomes of each family member, this could reduce the motivation of the family breadwinner to urge his union to fight for a family wage.

This is a replay of the reaction of unions to the introduction of unconditional family allowances earlier this century. British trade unionists were not enamoured with the example of France, where a director of the French Family Allowance Fund had claimed that 'the payment of family allowances has prevented trade unions from making use of family men for helping in their revolutionary aims and the majority of family men among workers have remained outside the class struggle.'[5] But some, such as Hugh Dalton, argued that unions would be strengthened: 'Imagine the effect which the possession of this steady income would have had upon both the men's power to resist the employers' demands and upon the attitude of the employers themselves.'[6]

Bill Jordan has argued[7] that the trade union objection to basic income is archaic. If the aim of trade unions is to maintain the living standards of the working class, then unions must abandon their nineteenth century assumptions that wages determine household income and that maintaining the wage levels of full-time male employees is the most effective way to maintain the living standards of the working class. With massive government involvement already in the labour market, in planning employment and in fixing net income through manipulation of tax and welfare levels, it is not true that wages are the sole determinant of take-home pay. As Table 2 in Chapter Four demonstrates, for those whose wages are around the poverty level in the UK, net income is determined not by wages but by the tax/benefit system. Fighting for higher wages for those in the poverty trap may even worsen their lot! It is first necessary to reform the tax/benefit system if wage-bargaining for the low paid (or indeed a national minimum wage) is to have any point at all, and basic income provides just such a reform that will once again give point to wage bargaining.

A second, related union objection is that basic income will lead to wages going down. But in our modern world in which net income is determined by the interaction of wages, taxes and benefits, surely most people are more concerned about how much their household has at the end of the day than about gross wages. Basic income schemes such as BIG 1(a) will leave families with children up to average earnings or even above with more than at present. Those groups who have traditionally not been represented by unions (non-earning households and part-time female earners) stand particularly to gain with basic income.

There is a debate within the left as to whether a national minimum wage is desirable; some argue for it as a guarantee that wages cannot fall below a certain level, others argue against it on the ground that wage levels should be fixed by collective bargaining, not legislation[8]. Some on the left therefore oppose basic income proposals that would abolish existing minimum wage legislation, as would Keith Roberts' proposal. However, there is a debate among basic income advocates themselves as to the desirability of a minimum wage[9]. Although the free market argument for basic income would seem logically to entail abolishing minimum wage legislation, there are many other rationales for basic income, several of which could include a minimum wage. The Dutch WRR report advocated the abolition of the legal minimum wage, but one of its architects, Dr. N.H. Douben, later clarified that they meant the reduction of the minimum wage only by the amount of the basic income, thus leaving earners with the same guarantee of minimum income that they currently enjoy.[10] Clearly there is scope for debate here. It seems to me that the key question for unions is not just whether they are going to support basic income but more importantly whether they are going to get involved in the debate and influence basic income thinking. There is nothing in socialist theory that makes basic income taboo, in fact the reverse; it would be tragic for the labour movement if a basic income scheme were introduced and the unions had not been involved in its conception.

The objection to basic income on the grounds that it may lead to some wages going down clearly is not justifiable in defense of working class living standards, which would undoubtedly go up under basic income! What then is the root of the objection about declining wage levels? I think it can only be a mystical belief in the dignity of wage labour, especially full-time male wage labour. Hilary Land[11] claims this was quite explicit in union objections to family allowances, and I have certainly come across it in the objections of ordinary people to basic income. Personally I very much believe in the value of labour, but I am not at all clear why paid labour should have more value and dignity than the unpaid labour of housework, schoolwork, voluntary work and caring for dependent children and relatives, all of which are important for the maintenance of living standards. And what dignity is there for the breadwinner in the poverty trap, or the would-be breadwinner in the unemployment trap? Table 2 in Chapter Four shows there is more dignity to be found in labour for the worker on less than average earnings under BIG 1(a) than under the present British system.

One final objection from trade unionists is that they would rather rely on their own wage negotiations than on the beneficence of the state. Back in the 1920s, Ernest Bevin was against letting living standards become dependent on family allowances whose value would be determined not by unions but by a possibly Conservative government[12]. This is a real danger, as discussed in my section on 'Preventing Poverty', but we have to face up to the reality that take-home wages are already determined by government. Converting tax exemptions and welfare payments into a basic income does not alter that.

In conclusion, Jordan's analysis suggests that the objections to basic income typically made by trade unions have two things in common. First, the objections are neither socialist nor based on defending the interests and living standards of the working class. Rather, the objections are deeply traditional, based on traditional notions of the supremacy of the full-time male employee. They are deeply hierarchical in that they seek to preserve the old order, with dependents who have not earned benefits kept as second class citizens and with the breadwinning husband the king of his own home.

Secondly, the objections are out of touch with reality. Things have changed enormously since earlier days of unionism in which full male employment reigned. There are now women in paid work in vast numbers, often part-time, and most of the poor are to be found in the increasing numbers of households with no earners at all — the unemployed and pensioner households. These form the new lower class which has been entirely left out of the prizes on offer to the heavyweights of organized labour and employers[13]. It is significant that socialist advocates of basic income have come from precisely this new proletariat — from the unions of claimants and unemployed, from a few trade unions representing the low paid, and from women.

The new class divide

Both the neo-Marxist argument for basic income in terms of propertied capitalist versus propertyless workers, and the objections from trade unions, are out of date. Both pretend we are living in a Victorian early capitalist world that is now largely gone, not least because of the efforts of trade unions themselves. Socialists have to re-think class analysis.

Van Parijs[14] considers basic income thoroughly appropriate to what he calls 'the new class divide'. He observes three historical stages. In feudalism, the basic divide was between landowners and the landless. In industrial capitalism, the divide was between owners of the means of production and workers. But now an unemployed class has become a permanent feature of welfare state capitalism, and the main divide in this third stage is between jobholders and the jobless. Along with race and sex, it is now jobs that are the real basis of class. The divide today between jobholders and jobless is as real as was the Victorian divide between gentlemen and labourers.

Both Marxist theorists and practical trade unionists are overwhelmingly members of the jobholding class. Conceptually, their ideas are stuck in the second stage of classical capitalism: their traditional preoccupation with the fight against the bosses conveniently (for them) diverts attention from the new class struggle. Certainly many unemployed and sub-employed today know that neither trade unionism nor Marxist theory have much to offer them. What use is the fight against the bosses or the fight for higher pay when you haven't even got a job?

Vis-a-vis capital, workers and their unions are the underdog, and therefore it should be possible to persuade them of the merits of basic income along the lines advocated earlier in this section. But vis-a-vis many housewives, part-time female workers and those prevented by disability and unemployment from earning, full-time skilled workers and their unions are distinctly privileged. Since basic income especially helps those with little or no attachment to paid employment, it could well help end the privileges of the skilled male worker and his union. It would end the present situation in which jobholders and the jobless are treated totally differently by the tax and welfare authorities, and offer solidarity between jobholder and jobless, skilled employee and dependent housewife, that is as radical as efforts would have been in Victorian times to put gentleman and labourer on an equal footing. Even if some trade unionists and some labour parties oppose basic income, true socialists who believe in equality and solidarity have to take it seriously.

Some of the leading advocates of basic income, at least in the UK, argue for it because it will provide an independent income for women[1]. Their argument is a natural extension of the arguments for freedom and equality of the previous two sections. I suggested that the simple Marxist two-class picture of propertied capitalists versus propertyless workers needs to be updated; certainly it fails to capture the experience of many women. The updated version with which I concluded the previous section could be restated as a three-class picture[2]: 1) There are those with property who need not sell their labour power (this includes women of property who need not themselves look after their children but can pay someone else to care for them). 2) There are those without property who have to sell their labour power if they are to subsist, and who have the right and opportunity to do so (men with paid jobs, and women without dependent children and with paid jobs). Though this group has little freedom vis-a-vis the constraints of the world of employment, it does have considerable power vis-a-vis the third group: 3) These are those without property who are denied the opportunity and/or the right to sell their labour power, and who therefore have to remain dependent on a husband or on state welfare. (Many wives and mothers, and the unemployed and disabled.) Members of this group are indeed third class, unable to make decisions in their own right. Being bottom of a three-tier heap can be worse than being at the bottom of a two-tier heap. Those in the second tier, feeling powerless vis-a-vis the first tier may compensate by lording it over the third tier. The petty bank clerk or the alienated manual worker restores his feeling of manliness by becoming a tyrant at home; or resentful and overtaxed employees vote in governments that punish the unemployed.

In the section on 'Preventing Poverty', I described the poverty that can afflict the economically dependent wife; for many it is the loss of freedom as much as the poverty that hurts. Even if a wife is given enough money or gifts in kind by her husband to live at a reasonable standard of living, the fact of having like a child to ask his permission for everything is often experienced as intolerable by women living in a society that claims to value personal liberty and the freedom of opinion of the individual. The humiliation, the loss of confidence and self-worth, and the resentment felt so acutely by many unemployed men today have long been felt by wives who have been denied access to the dignity of paid labour most of their married lives[3].

A universal basic income, given to every individual, attacks at source both the economic poverty and the lack of liberty of the dependent wife. This has perhaps not been better put than by Lady Rhys-Williams who wrote in 1953 that the most important advantage of her social dividend scheme 'is the help, small as it is, which it offers to those women who are still living as slaves in the midst of our free society — the wives of mean or broken men who give them no money to spend at their own discretion and little enough upon which to provide food and clothing for the family, but from whose tyranny they cannot escape without abandoning their children.'[4] Basic income would, to a certain degree, transform the dependent wife into a woman of independent means, with the possibility of thinking and acting on her own, just as her husband can. This is not to say that an independent income will automatically end the more subtle forms of dependence, but it is an important first step.

If basic income provides an independent income for women, it also helps provide a just and equitable framework within which women and men may negotiate how to live their lives. At present in most western nations, there is a bizarre array of government-sponsored incentives and intrusions based on gender and marital status. In Britain, the married man's tax allowance provides an unnecessary bonus for marriage, whereas it is parenthood that typically incurs extra costs. Many countries grant social assistance to a non-earning single mother but not to a non-earning married or cohabiting mother, thus creating an incentive to split or not to marry or remarry.

The only way of eradicating these anomalies is to abolish personal tax exemptions and go for a cashable tax credit given to, and income tax levied on, the individual, not the household. In other words, basic income. Such a scheme is completely neutral between men/women, between marriage/cohabitation/living alone, and between earners/non-earners. Men and women can therefore make choices about how they wish to live and work, based on their own values, commitments and desires without having to take into account financial incentives that all too often were cooked up in a previous generation when values, and certainly economic conditions, were very different.

I will explore the implications of basic income firstly for women's paid employment, and secondly for the forming and breaking of family units.

Women's employment

In the section on automation, I argued that basic income could give real teeth to the right to earn. It would provide a real choice for people who at present have little choice: either we have to work, or we are forced into unwilling and poverty-stricken idleness. Basic income would change that.

Some readers may have been thinking of men at this point, but it is married women who will probably most feel the force of this basic income manifesto for work. Many wives who would like to go out and earn a decent income in a skilled job are unable to do so because of the low wages offered, the lack of child care, or the patriarchal attitude of their husbands; both the financial and the emotional economics add up to him working overtime and her staying at home to make apple pie and woolly jumpers for the kids. Other women who would rather stay home to look after their children may have to go out to work in order to make ends meet. In each case, economics and archaic laws conspire to prevent her living according to her own values. She does not have autonomy.

How will basic income enable women to go out to work who now find it difficult? Apart from discrimination in the labour market and sheer lack of jobs, the major problem at present is the care of children or other dependent relatives; finding someone else to care while out at work may be difficult, and paying them more difficult still. The basic incomes of the parents, their children and/or any other dependent relatives can, in part or in whole, be used to pay for care. This will not in itself make such care available but, if sufficient women offer to pay, then fee-charging provision, private or public, is likely to increase. Basic income could provide extra leverage for those fighting for more child care facilities, and authorities unwilling at present to subsidize child-care fully could well be induced to provide partially subsidized facilities.

Another reason in Britain why some wives do not go out to work when they want to, and even when their husbands want them to, is the rules governing income support for unemployed men. These state that if not only the unemployed husband but also his wife earns more than £5 per week, then this will be deducted pound for pound from the benefit. So there is little point in his wife either taking or continuing legal paid employment. The *General Household Survey* of 1982 found that, whereas 59% of employed husbands had a working wife, only 29% of unemployed husbands had a wife who admitted to working outside the home. There are various reasons for this difference[5], but the social assistance rules are certainly a factor. This illustrates how *selective* benefits based on *household* needs distort things in a way that not only alarms free market theorists but can also cause considerable restrictions, unhappiness and poverty in ordinary households. Basic incomes given to the individual, whatever the circumstances, simply do not have this kind of perverse effect, and will give women in households containing an unemployed man the same choice of whether or not to work enjoyed by their more fortunate sisters. This is another example of how basic income enhances the incentive to earn of precisely those individuals who most need it.

Britain, and doubtless other countries too, is increasingly divided into households with two or more earners who are getting by or better, and households with no earners. It seems extraordinary that, just when the poverty of long-term unemployment for the chief earner begins to bite, so the spouse may also be forced to give up earning (or be forced into dishonesty). Basic income would not only add directly to the income of earner-less households, but would also make it worthwhile for wives to take employment if it is available. If in so doing basic income increases the number of one-earner (that is, female earner) households, then it will be a victory for fairness, for equality between the sexes and between households, and for freedom of choice.

At the same time as helping to remove the obstacles currently preventing some wives from earning, basic income will also give women more freedom to cease paid work should that be their choice. It provides a buffer against the poverty that is currently driving many mothers or less than wholly fit women into low-paying work, and gives them the option to stay home. The evidence of the American negative income tax experiments is pertinent here, for many poorly paid women took advantage of guaranteed income to stay home. Though some American critics see this as a mark against guaranteed income, inducing poor people into dependence on the state rather than into supporting themselves, it is clear to me that poor mothers do not retire from paid work in order to put their feet up and watch T.V. It seems to me more likely that guaranteed income gave them a buffer against poverty and enabled them to organize their lives and look after their children more effectively. A basic income scheme might well have this effect, though an important point in favour of basic income is that, unlike negative income tax, it does not give *more* to those who decide to cease earning. It treats earners and non-earners evenly.

As well as being freer to choose whether they wish to earn, women will also be freer to choose whether to earn full-time or part-time. In Britain, nearly half of female employees work part-time. One reason is the small universal child benefit, which lets many off having to work full-time but not enough to cease work altogether; another is the first £2,000 of earnings being free of tax and social security contributions, above which level the net value of earning declines sharply. Basic income will in effect raise child benefits, and at the same time levy an even rate of tax on all earnings (up to a certain point, which few women are in present conditions likely to reach). It will abolish some of the current inducements (for employers as well as employees) to part-time earning, and women will therefore be able to choose, unconstrained by tax and welfare rules, whether to earn full-time, part-time, or not at all. Just as will young people, old people, indeed any people.

Women's wages

So far, I have been exploring the options that basic income will present to married and cohabiting women. One conclusion is certain: basic income will give women more options whether, and how much, to earn. If a woman earns, it will be more because she has chosen to and less because she has to. Another conclusion seems very probable: considerably more women will choose to cease formal paid employment than will choose to start work or increase their hours at work. What then will be the overall effect of perhaps hundreds of thousands of women making this decision? Two scenarios seem possible.

First is the optimistic scenario. In the short term, many women will withdraw from paid employment, especially from part-time employment. A few may shift from part-time to full-time. This will create a shortage of the cheap female labour that many employers have exploited for so long. In the longer run, this will provide a powerful incentive for employers to raise women's wages, to improve terms and conditions, and to give part-time workers the same perks that full-time workers currently enjoy. Women will return to work in similar numbers to today, but with better pay and conditions and with more choice as to the number of hours they work. In other words, basic income will provide a framework of equality and fairness which will eliminate the incentives that currently cause employers to pay women less than men. Basic income will do more for equal opportunities and equal pay for women in the UK than two decades of legislation has achieved. This legislation has done less than had been hoped because it has not changed the tax allowances and social security contribution rules that have underlain the exploitation of low-paid workers. Basic income forms the base upon which equal pay legislation can become effective.

Now the pessimistic scenario. Part-time workers, most of whom are women, are currently in the unique position of not having to pay tax, nor in some countries social security contributions, on their earnings. With basic income, they will be faced with paying income tax on all earnings. Since their present employers are not always the most scrupulous or honourable, the women will be offered, and accept, cash under the table. They will not declare their earnings to the tax authority, and low wages will continue. Since the women as well as the employer will be breaking the law, the women will be unable to resist worsening conditions and will lose protection under the law.

I do not deny this pessimistic scenario could happen, but if equality for the sexes in the workplace is to stand any chance, then all workers must be treated equally by the law. So long as, at present, part-time women workers do not have to pay tax, and full-time workers — female and male — do, then there is little hope for decent wages or conditions for workers in those occupations currently dominated by part-time female labour. If sex equality is to stand a chance, we must go for basic income, and then take whatever measures are necessary to prevent the pessimistic scenario.

Feminist objections

Although some of the leading advocates of basic income have been women concerned with financial independence for their own sex, the women's movement has generally remained either ignorant about or hostile to basic income. I hope the lack of knowledge about basic income is being remedied. But why the hostility?

The women's movement has identified the economic dependence of women on men as a root problem, and has fought to end discrimination in the labour market and to set up childcare facilities so that women can go out and earn on equal terms with men. Women's own earnings are seen as the remedy for dependence. Feminists typically have distrusted government handouts to women who work at home, believing these to be an unreliable gift: public patriarchy is no more to be trusted than private patriarchy. As Carol Brown puts it, 'Public patriarchy increases the power of higher level men over all women and decreases the power of lower level men over any woman.'[6] Welfare payments are typically legislated for by well-off men and given to poor women. If women particularly stand to gain from basic income, will it not be just another form of public patriarchy? The wife's income will depend less on her own husband, and more on a remote, usually male, legislator. Just as trade unionists would rather battle with an employer they can see and negotiate with, so many women would rather fight that employer for decent wages or even cajole more money out of their husbands, both targets they can at least see.

I think the feminist hostility or caution concerning basic income is also due to a certain assumption that, earnings apart, getting a woman out of the confines of the home into the public world of employment enables her to grow in confidence and learn how to change the balance of power within society at large. Otherwise, she will be left at home, fighting rearguard skirmishes in a war the married woman has already lost.

Feminists within the basic income movement have argued, however that, far from undermining their efforts towards liberation, basic income would actually enhance them. The following points seem pertinent.

1) It is doubtful that going out to work necessarily makes women more politically active. It is certainly true that some women have become politically aware through trade unionism, but as many if not more women are involved in local politics precisely because they do not have to go out to work and therefore have the time and energy to do political work. The early feminists were middle class non-earners, often with an independent income of their own. In the United States, more women become politically aware through their churches than through their trade unions. This is not to doubt the value of paid work, but simply to doubt the claim that it is an essential part of any strategy of raising women's awareness and political clout.

2) Any short-term retreat of wives from paid work to live on basic income could well be followed by a longer-term revival first of wage levels and then of women going back into the labour force. As has been argued consistently throughout this book, contrary to some public opinion, basic income could aid rather than hamper employment policies.

3) Many feminists did indeed resist the introduction of family allowances in the 1920s and 1930s, on the grounds that they would be used by husbands to keep their wives in their place at home. Hitler used family allowances for precisely that purpose. However, there is no evidence that family allowances have prevented mothers from taking paid employment in other countries, and indeed in the UK feminists have become great supporters of child benefit.

4) Because everyone would receive basic income, there will be substantial political pressure, from both men and women, to

maintain its value. It could even become a political sacred cow, like mortgage interest tax relief, which no government at present would dare abolish. Several basic income schemes would be unlike any welfare benefit in that more than half the voters would gain, and such a scheme would therefore receive political support more akin to personal tax allowances than welfare benefits.

5) Finally, if women *choose* to give up earning, what is so wrong with that?

Family life

What is the likely effect of basic income on the forming and splitting of households?

There are two things to consider here. One is that basic income provides an independent income for the wife and any dependent children or relatives, as well as for the husband. The other is that basic income, because it is given to the individual rather than to the household, favours neither living with others nor living by yourself. (Current social assistance, paid to each eligible household, subsidizes splitting.) Basic income allows the natural economies of scale involved in living with others, notably having to pay for only one dwelling, to operate. In other words, basic income might not provide enough for either partner to live on should they split and have to finance two separate households. It would reverse the clock to before the days when social assistance bailed out the divorcee, and the natural financial penalty of turning one household into two would once again operate.

For this reason advocates of basic income have had to think seriously about how divorced or separated partners in financial distress should be aided. In Parker's BIG 1(a), the income-tested housing benefit would provide the necessary extra assistance, and she has also considered a supplement for single parents. In some of her other schemes she includes a supplement for all householders, which would take care of the difference in cost between running one and two households. The precise effect of any actual basic income scheme on the incentive to marry, stay together, or split can only be judged, therefore, when it is known what kind and level of extra assistance would be available to single parents.

Overall, though, the same principle would operate with household formation as would operate with employment: lack of interference in people's lives so that they can choose to live according to their own values, preferences and sense of duty. Just as basic income would sweep away the vast array of incentives and disincentives that encourage some people to do paid work and others not, irrespective of their own preferences, so it would also sweep away the bizarre rewards and penalties for various forms of household.

Many of these rewards and penalties were put in place in previous generations when circumstances and values were different from now. For example, the UK married man's allowance was instituted when most taxpayers were middle class males and when middle class wives did not do paid work, so marriage for a taxpayer involved adding a dependent to his household and he was therefore allowed this extra tax allowance. Now, though, almost all employees pay tax, and the vast majority of women continue working after marriage, so that marriage adds an extra income rather than a dependent; it is parenthood that brings extra costs today. The 1990 reform of UK income tax toward independent taxation for spouses will not change this. The new married couple allowance still provides a bonus for marriage rather than parenthood.

There are other perverse effects of special allowances for married people. If you invite a member of the opposite sex to marry you and live with you, you, as a couple, get a big tax bonus; if you invite your ailing granny to live with you, you do not. Other rewards and penalties are simply unintended consequences of tax and social security measures designed for other purposes. The result, though, is the same. Especially if your finances are tight, it can be difficult to live according to your values and preferences, and you are pressed to arrange your household according to tax/benefit rules instead. Who can want that?

Just as basic income can appeal to both left and right, so it seems to me that it could appeal both to feminists and to traditional upholders of the family. At present, tax/benefit rules neither respect the right of women to choose how to live, nor in several instances do they allow without penalty a normal family life. Neither feminists nor traditionalists can be happy with this. Basic income would enable feminists to live as they choose, and traditionalists to live without penalty the kind of family life they believe to be right. For each individual and for each family, basic income would return the question about how to live to the proper realm of values and choices; manipulation of or by tax/benefit rules would thankfully become obsolete.

6. viii. An independent income for those needing care

Throughout, I have argued that basic income is most in the interest of those individuals who have little or no income through their own labour power. This means the low paid, the unemployed, the elderly, housewives — and those needing to be looked after by others because of tender years, sickness or disability. Though these may be dearly loved by those who care for them, they are nevertheless dependent, vulnerable and powerless. If they are not adequately loved, they have little else to fall back on. Would not an independent income for them be in their interest?

Childhood

In poor countries which have a strong tradition of the extended family, it is quite common for children to spend much of their time staying with various relatives, either because they have developed a particular relationship with the child, or because they live near the school the child attends, or because the child has been orphaned, or whatever. One reason children can benefit from the care of more distant relatives, or even neighbours, is that it does not cost much to bring up a child in such societies. If anything, the child may well bring in income to the family through its own labour.

One reason, perhaps, that nuclear families in the West seem to get more and more isolated is that it is so expensive bringing up a child in our society that, quite simply, I cannot afford to have relatives' children living under my roof, and their parents cannot afford to pay me. Basic income would begin to change that. Though it would not be sufficient to make up for the wages lost through having children, nor pay for full-time professional child-care, it would reimburse a relative or neighbour who already had children for the extra food and clothing consumed by the extra child.

The child's basic income is technically its own, and could be paid into its own bank account. It could be used to negotiate which adults the child should live with. This might seem a denial of parental rights in a society such as ours in which children are believed by parents to be some kind of possession, but it would not seem at all strange in societies based on the extended family. We may perhaps have something to learn from them.

Disability

Certainly acceptable, however, would be the increased freedom of choice that basic income would give those unable to live independently because of disability or frailty in old age. They would have more power themselves to choose who is to look after them[1]. At present, if they are not sufficiently incapacitated to go into institutional care, they are usually lumbered with whichever relative is prepared to put up with the hard and often emotionally draining work of looking after them. The elderly or disabled person may have little choice in the matter but to be grateful. If they were receiving a basic income augmented because of age or disability, they could use this, if not actually to pay the caring relative of their choice, then at least to ensure that the often considerable extra expense is reimbursed and to pay for the occasional 'grannysitter' to give the family a night off. This could well open up to the person requiring care a range of friends, relatives and neighbours who might otherwise be unable financially to cope with them, and it would certainly leave the cared-for person with more dignity. This in turn would mean that the uncounted army of women who look after relatives at home would themselves have that bit more status and spare time and be less out of pocket. It might also to some extent help children in the appalling position of having to look unaided after a disabled parent. Just as basic income frees wives and husbands to negotiate the terms of co-operation without duress from tax/benefit regulations, so it helps free those with a disability and those caring for them to negotiate with dignity the terms of co-operation.

There are various ways in which basic income could be geared for carers and those they care for. Hermione Parker has suggested that the person with the disability should receive a Disability Costs Allowance, whose value would depend on the degree of disability, while the carer should receive a supplement equal to the normal old-age supplement. This raises the question of how 'full-time caring' is to be defined? Should it include those with young children to look after, the cost would become astronomical.

Bill Jordan has suggested that the person with the disability should receive a Disability Costs Allowance at a level adequate to pay for care, however expensive that might be. The person could then buy any combination of family, neighbourly, commercial, contract or public care, according to their choice. This would clearly cost a lot, and would be paid by taxpayers — virtually all of whom are lucky enough to be neither disabled nor asked to care full time for someone who is.

With any such basic income supplement geared to the degree of disability, there are the thorny questions of who determines this and how? Presumably this would have to be by some combination of medical certificate and proven inability to earn. But what redress would there be for those who believe they are disabled from earning but whose doctors say they are not? How would malingerers be weeded out? How is the effect of disability on earning potential to be assessed by a medical expert who has little or no special knowledge of the labour market?

If inability to earn is the main reason for providing a basic income supplement, then why should the elderly receive a supplement simply because they have reached a fixed age? If as

I have suggested the concept of a fixed retirement age should disappear, and since basic income is based on need and permanent residence in a country rather than entitlement via contributions, then why should those over a given age receive a supplement? That they have 'earned' it is no part of basic income thinking. One solution would be for supplements to be paid simply on the ground of inability to work, so that the old person would, like anyone else, have to produce medical certification that they are unable to earn. In effect, old age pensions would be replaced entirely by disablement supplements. Though this would be consistent with the philosophy of basic income, there would be initial resistance because old age pensions are politically highly popular. It might be wiser initially to propose an age supplement, or progressive age supplements, as a replacement for current state pensions.

This whole area of support for those physically or mentally unable to supplement their basic income by earning is a thorny one and requires detailed discussion with the pensioner and disability lobbies before a costed basic income scheme can be formally presented to the public. In the UK, this kind of discussion is already going on and the problems are being worked through.[2] It is fair to add that the problems are no less thorny for those who propose reform along more conventional lines, nor indeed for those who have to live with the present system.

The goal though is clear. Those adults requiring care should have an unconditional and adequate income that enables them to make the kind of choices that the rest of us take for granted. Both they and their carers should be able to relate to each other and the outside world with dignity. Basic income would play a part in bringing this about.

Liberty, equality, fraternity. If some argue for basic income in the name of liberty, and some in the name of reducing economic inequalities, some also stress its potential for helping to restore fraternity, or social harmony and fellowship among citizens. This is perhaps even more difficult to attain and more fragile to maintain in complex modern societies than either liberty or a measure of economic equality. It certainly seems to have fewer people and parties waving its banner.

All too often, citizens achieve a sense of oneness through villifying other nations, as in jingoism, or in villifying one particular nation, as in a cold war. Sometimes war itself is actually welcomed, bringing a heightened sense of national unity. Britain, during the 1982 Falklands War, demonstrated this all too clearly. Or workmates or neighbours gain a sense of solidarity by denigrating or joking about blacks, queers, and other despised groups. When economic prosperity or social harmony are frail, citizens are only too willing to be offered scapegoats. H.D. Duncan wrote in 1962, referring to the purges of Stalin and Hitler, 'The fact of victimage, so terribly obvious in our time, must be accepted and studied. Any social theory that does not take into account the terrible fact that men "need" each other to satisfy their hate, as well as their love, becomes singularly irrelevant to a generation that has lived in the world of Hitler.'[1] How may this unhealthy, but all too common, way of gaining a sense of national or group unity be turned into a more healthy sense of participation in a community in which we are all interdependent and in which all co-operate for the common good even as we as individuals pursue our own personally chosen projects?

One particular division that is likely to lead to scapegoating is tax/welfare arrangements that divide people into the worthy and the unworthy. One person is deemed to have earned his income as 'earnings' or pensions paid for out of earnings, while another is reminded she is a burden on the taxpayer who has to pay for her welfare benefits. In the UK, unemployed claimants are often identified in the popular press as 'scroungers', thus boosting a sense of self-righteousness in the ordinary worker and taxpayer as the economy collapses around him, and helping to elect and maintain Mrs. Thatcher's government[2]. A new sense of social cohesion was bought for some at the expense of those unfortunate enough to be labelled 'burdens on society'.

As well as being villified, unemployed claimants can all too easily find themselves in a position of 'structural guilt' in which they are declared guilty irrespective of their personal behaviour. I have mentioned how if they, or even sometimes their wives, manage to earn more than a very few pounds doing an odd job they will lose the same amount in benefit, and some may find themselves disqualified from benefit altogether simply because they are doing voluntary work and cannot therefore be seriously seeking paid employment. Their choice is either to stay at home depressed or to be active but to deceive the authorities. Since human beings are, I believe by nature, active and creative, and since unemployed claimants often desperately need the money or the esteem that comes from working, many respond by working on the side and not telling the authorities. They are virtually forced by the system into dishonesty, into guilt. When one relatively small section of the population is placed in this position, then the stage has been well and truly set for the majority gaining their sense of self-worth by 'blaming the victim'.

For some, a major reason for basic income is that it would provide a basis for healing some of these wounds. Placing workers and non-workers within the same basic income system, though a stumbling block to some critics, is for others the source of its healing potential. It would replace structural guilt with a universal structure of acceptance and forgiveness[3]. With increasing polarization between right and left in many western nations, and the possibility of continuing alienation between employed and unemployed, restoring social harmony is important if western civilization is to survive. It very nearly didn't, for just this cause, forty-five years ago.

We must be clear what we mean by social cohesion[4]. Lack of cohesion can mean overt hostility between groups, or it can mean isolation and lack of any relation at all between groups. And are we talking of the relation between taxpayer and claimant, employer and employee, or between family members? A scheme such as basic income could conceivably aid cohesion in one sense and damage it in another. Those, such as Bill Jordan, who advocate basic income on grounds of social harmony, are usually thinking of reducing hostility between taxpayers and claimants, and it is in this sense that I will begin my discussion. Later in this section, I will ask whether basic income, though reducing overt hostility, may not at the same time promote isolation between citizens and particularly between family members.

Claimants and taxpayers

In all Western nations during the late 1960s and 1970s, the proportion of gross national product going to social security benefits increased substantially, paid for mainly by increasing taxation on middle income earners and extending taxation to low income earners. This created a climate in which ordinary people on below average earnings began to feel resentful of what they experienced as a heavy tax burden, and in some countries they began to vent their anger on those receiving social assistance, such as long-term unemployed males (in the UK) or black single mothers (in the USA). These were convenient scapegoats, and in the USA few wanted to know that most of the increase on spending had gone on social insurance benefits such as pensions and relatively little on income-tested benefits. In the UK, there had indeed been a shift toward reliance on income-tested supplementary benefit, as a cheap way of coping with increased financial need.

The healing potential claimed for basic income is that, as it is for everyone, it abolishes the distinction between taxpayer and claimant, in the same way that universal education and the national health service do. At some stage in my life I am a net contributor, but at other stages I have been or will be a net recipient. Similarly with basic income. Although some people will at this moment be net contributors, there will be stages in their lives when they are not earning and they or their family will be glad they are receiving basic income. Further, citizens will no more have to 'claim' basic income than they have to 'claim' education for their children.

One way in which the UK is divided at present is that social security fraud is investigated more assiduously and with greater invasion of privacy than is income tax fraud. Social security claimants often find themselves existing within a structure of guilt, with clerks and inspectors often assuming them to be on the fiddle. Taxpayers, by contrast, exist within a structure of forgiveness, and are not routinely checked for fraud. Inland Revenue staff are overworked, so haven't time to check up on everyone. Social security staff are also overworked, but the UK government provides special funds to boost fraud detection. The advantage of a basic income scheme that unites tax and social security administration is that all citizens, if investigated, will be investigated by the same department, within the same climate of trust or distrust. If the climate is one of unfounded distrust, it will offend so many voters that there will be pressure for it to be changed. More important, since there will be no work test attached to basic income, there will be less reason to conceal earnings from the authorities and the main source of social security fraud (claiming while working) will automatically end.

Basic income would be a tangible sign that all are full members of society. Ours is a productive society in which all should have the opportunity to work, but it is also a consumer society from which many are excluded either by household poverty or by the lack of their own personal income. Since basic income would enable all to receive an income without stigma, it would enable all to participate. Whatever you may think of the consumer society, it leads to social division for some to be excluded, or to be included only on humiliating terms. If you have ever stood in line at a British supplementary benefit office, or noticed the look of the check-out girl in an American supermarket as you pay for your groceries with food stamps, then you know what it means to be excluded from participation with honour in the consumer society. In our materialistic society, it seems that you cannot be a full member unless you have earned your income. Basic income challenges that.

Objections

Basic income would help some to turn their backs on the productive and reproductive units which sustain them to a far greater extent than now[5]. Taxpayers who do not share the ethic of maximizing freedom for all will undoubtedly perceive rapid transition to a full basic income scheme as legalizing social and economic parasitism. As one critic has written recently[6], 'What feasible prospect is there of the working population being persuaded to reduce their present standards of consumption not in the interests of providing useful work for all, but in order to raise the living standards of those *voluntarily* out of work . . . Why should individuals have a right to equal shares if they are unwilling in principle to make an equal commitment to the social good?' Although current work tests and means tests are stigmatizing and foster cynicism and perverse incentives, they may nevertheless be effective in keeping the fear of social parasitism somewhat at bay.

Although basic income aims to abolish the distinction between taxpayer and claimant, at the same time it might vividly reinforce the distinction between net contributor and net beneficiary. Currently in the welfare state, redistribution is supposed to be from the lucky and well-endowed to the unlucky and disadvantaged, not from the industrious to the lazy. Basic income redistributes from those who perform paid work to those who do not. Though this need not involve redistribution from the industrious to the lazy (because many beneficiaries may be disabled, involuntarily unemployed, or do a lot of useful unpaid work), the possibility is obvious to all.

Virtually all work is painful as well as pleasurable. Subconsciously, and sometimes consciously, we are ambivalent about work. This ambivalence is reflected in every major European language in which the word *labour* connotes burden, pain and the pangs of childbirth as well as a chief activity through which humans fulfill themselves, serve one another and gain dignity[7]. This places a question mark against whether it is really worth labouring to gain more than subsistence, especially if my labour is particularly hard, boring or harmful to others. Many of us avoid facing this question through the psychological processes of splitting and projection, in which all my good feelings about labour I attach to myself (perhaps by adopting the work ethic and gaining pride in supporting my family, even as I make arms or cigarettes that kill others), and all the bad feelings I project onto those who apparently choose not to work. Since with a full basic income there will be no hiding the possibility that some have chosen not to take paid work, this kind of hostility toward the unemployed could continue, even thrive.

In the USA, the hostility is likely to be toward black single mothers. The past two decades have witnessed a move of many an American wife from the home range to work in office or factory, in order to maintain living standards. This was often after much soul-searching and opposition from families in which wives had stayed home for generations; the new working wife therefore justifies her choice by espousing the work ethic vociferously. Whereas a previous generation may have been happy for welfare mothers to be at home looking after their kids, the modern working American wife or working single mother is damned if she's going to pay for the welfare mother to enjoy what she herself can no longer enjoy. Again, if basic income leads to more poor mothers staying home, and if many of them are identifiable as black, then such hostility could continue.

However, if employers respond with flexibility, many people would realize that the choice is not between continuing to work thirty-five or forty hours or opting out, but that earnings from fewer hours plus basic income add up to a life that more suits themselves and their families. If this wider choice of hours becomes available with basic income, then there is a real chance that society will not be divided into ambivalent earners versus subsistence-line opters-out, but become a harmonious whole in which for the first time since the industrial revolution the ordinary person regains control over the hours s/he works[8].

Whether basic income would foster social harmony would depend on whether it is accompanied by not only more flexible working hours but also a whole range of other institutional changes. The abolition of retirement and school leaving ages, and increased provision for ongoing education, I have already mentioned. Another would be an infrastructure that is more geared to work being done in the home and local community as well as in factory and office; this might involve houses being designed differently (at present, architects unrealistically assume that the kitchen is the only room in which work is carried out) and the ending or changing of zoning laws. With these changes, the pessimistic scenario of ambivalent earners versus subsistence-line opters-out might be avoided, and an optimistic scenario become reality in which all recognize the different kinds of work in which citizens engage.

Isolation

Basic income, by its very nature, is radically individualistic in two senses: a) by not being conditional on gender, marital status or paid employment, it enlarges the individual's sphere of freedom; b) single individuals rather than households become the unit of entitlement and taxation. Even if basic income were to reduce hostility between certain sections of the population, would this be at the cost of eroding relationships of any kind? Would conflict be replaced by isolation?

Michael Ignatieff in his brilliant essay 'The Needs of Strangers'[9] argues that the welfare state enables people to accept financial and other support from others precisely because it is impersonal, and does not carry the obligations that help from kin carries. To some extent, basic income will reduce the personal giving of cash from husbands to wives, maybe even from parents to children, and replace this by the impersonal basic income; it will therefore further the process which Ignatieff suggests is already well developed: the market-initiated impersonal cash transaction. The welfare state takes depersonalization further, and basic income would take it further still. This may be welcomed by some wives and some older children (such as students), but what of Ignatieff's price? — 'The bureaucratized transfer of income among strangers has freed each of us from the enslavement of gift relations. Yet if the welfare state does serve the needs of freedom, it does not serve the needs of solidarity. We remain a society of strangers.'

The welfare state may well, I think, have increased a sense of solidarity among citizens who appreciate the implicit contract in which we all protect the welfare of each. It has ended the patriarchal relations that once governed the doling out of charity from the aristocracy to the labouring classes, and indeed some argue for basic income in order to end the patriarchal relations that still operate between breadwinning husbands and dependent wives. But would independence also bring a loss of obligation and consequent isolation?

Some critics fear precisely this. 'The idea of the guaranteed wage seems to be that it should be independent of obligations or contribution of any kind. The good society — the model is implicitly anarchist — is one in which no citizen is under any obligation to do anything at all.'[10] Some writings on basic income are quite clear that this is indeed the aim. Niels Meyer, for example: 'The basic income ... shall allow all Danish citizens to arrange their lives according to their own desires, independent of constraints from an undesired job — or from undesired ties to other human beings.'[11] In Henrietta's case, described in section ii of this chapter, freedom under basic income from the restraints imposed by an impenetrable social security maze and an irresponsible ex-husband, would lead to nothing but good. But it is also possible to imagine someone who views marital vows or rearing their own children as 'undesired ties to other human beings' and who would use basic income to escape from such ties. Barbara Ehrenreich has argued that from the 1950s onwards, even before the women's movement, American men lessened their commitment to breadwinning for their families[12]; their wives' basic income could provide a handy extra excuse.

However, as I have suggested several times before, the actual consequences of basic income may be very different from those first imagined. Paradoxically, it is by basing tax and welfare on the *individual* rather than the household that people can enjoy the natural economic advantages of living in family units rather than alone (section vii). And a generous basic income for those needing to be looked after could well lead to more people being cared for by relatives to their mutual satisfaction. Some might be able to fulfil felt duties and obligations toward sick kin that now either wear them out or that they cannot afford (section viii). If the economic consequences of basic income are difficult to predict, the personal and social consequences are that much more so. It would depend very much on the cultural and moral climate, and on complementary policies.

I am not happy with the individualist vision of all relationships being based on mutually agreed contracts. At the very least, it is an unavoidable fact that children do not contract with their parents to be born, and consequently it seems right that there should be ties, however 'undesired', that bind parents to children. Moreover, human groups — whether they be a couple, a village, a church, a trade union, or a nation — over time build up a reality of their own, which individuals are not free to renegotiate at will. And indeed, this group reality is the very source of the duty and commitment which give life meaning.

In the United States, where the language of individualism has become orthodoxy as never before in human history, people nevertheless retain deeply held commitments and obligations, even though their individualism fails to provide a language with which to describe these obligations[13]. The evidence of the USA, therefore, is that the language of radical individualism, of all relationships as negotiations between consenting partners, does not lead to the end of all social obligations. Far from it. What it does do is impoverish the language so that people cannot comprehend the commitments they actually have. The philosophy of basic income is far less single-mindedly individualist than American culture as a whole, for it explicitly includes fraternal and egalitarian aims as well as individualist aims to do with personal liberty. Personally, I would wish to see those advocating basic income maintain a healthy balance between these three aims.

A new Jeffersonian era?

In Chapter Six, I described how people committed to the free market, to socialism, and to feminism, have all argued that basic income is central to the fulfillment of each of their very different philosophies. I maintain that basic income could foster liberty, equality *and* fraternity:

In the pre-industrial era, there was more consensus on the key issue of property. When the United States were formed in the late eighteenth century, for example, democracy and freedom of thought were based on the non-slave household having title to its own piece of land. Jefferson believed there would be no freedom without private property, for without private property each man was the slave of his employer and of the currently accepted views of society. Even in England, ancient democratic rights stretching back to the early middle ages were effective in so far as they were based on the peasant household with rights to till or own certain pieces of land. But in an industrial society, few men and even fewer women enjoy this propertied base upon which democracy and personal freedom depend. Households and individuals now have no economic security other than a job from which they may be fired, a job guaranteed by political conformity to the state, state welfare with strings attached, or the beneficence of a husband; people can find their much-vaunted rights to personal liberty vacuous indeed.

Feminism, socialism and free-market political theory are all looking for a solution to this problem: how to preserve human autonomy in the context of the inevitably huge power of the modern state and of the modern enterprise?[1] The free marketeer believes that the unfettered right of the individual to acquire, hold and employ property is the only guarantee of freedom. The feminist points out that women are largely excluded from this by their rights to property having been expropriated by bourgeois husbands at the beginning of the capitalist era and by their exclusion from most of the riches of the labour market today. The socialist perceives the tyranny of large holdings of property to which capitalism naturally tends, and argues that all property must be held in common if the freedom and well-being of citizens is to be guaranteed.

Some free marketeers, some socialists and some feminists have perceived the limitations of their traditional solutions and proposed basic income as a key part of the way forward. They do this without ceasing to be free marketeers, socialists or feminists. But since the problem they are all addressing — how to preserve personal liberty when citizens cannot be Jeffersonian property owners — is essentially the same, it may well be that practical coalitions can be formed around the basic income proposal. What has divided these different ideologies has not been the goal (an Enlightenment vision of the free, prosperous citizen) but the means of reaching the goal. In basic income it seems possible they could agree on at least one of the means.

Basic income would provide a base for both the economic security so desired by socialism and by feminism, and the personal liberty and right to freedom of speech so desired by free marketeers and by feminism. Without independent means, the individual can rarely afford to dissent; basic income would help provide a basis for each individual. As Robert Theobald put it back in 1961, the guaranteed income 'could, at last, make Jefferson's ideal a reality in modern society by providing independent means, which would allow each individual to obtain minimum amounts of clothing, food, and shelter. They would not keep the family in luxury but would provide the necessities of life. The unemployed would be assured of a reasonable standard of living. The student, the writer, the artist, the visionary, the dissenter could live on this income if they considered their work sufficiently important.'[2]

For socialists, this vision of the good society stresses the freedom of the individual rather more than some socialists are used to. Individual freedom is, however, deeply valued by most members of advanced industrial societies, and socialists must come to terms with this. The merit of basic income is that it enables personal freedom to be experienced without depriving another of the means of subsistence or the freedom of thought. None can be deprived of basic income. Basic income provides a way of linking personal liberty with economic security, and could well be one key to developing an authentic modern socialism.

For free marketeers, basic income's stress on income rather than property may sound suspicious. However, advocates of people's capitalism (shareholdings for all) must appreciate that their vision of everyone becoming a significant shareholder is very far from becoming a reality. In the USA, the distribution of shares among the population is far more skewed than is the distribution of income[3]. In the UK, any increase in personal shareholdings that the Thatcher government may have induced is overshadowed by a huge contrary trend: the steady increase of pension funds and unit trusts, encouraged by the same government, which removes savings from the personal control of the individual and places them in the hands of vast financial houses who themselves decide where to invest the money.

Feminists have a strong commitment both to personal liberty and to economic equality (for some this means equality of opportunity, for others equality of outcome). Basic income would appear to foster liberty and both kinds of equality.

Personally, I am neither a card-carrying socialist nor an ideologically committed free-marketeer. Though I consider myself a fellow traveller with feminists, as a male I cannot claim membership of the women's movement. But I do have gut feelings about fairness, about equality, and about personal liberty, and an awareness that current disincentives against productive work, paid or unpaid, are absurd and cause individuals and families to suffer. I believe these gut feelings could make basic income attractive not only to free-marketeers, socialists and feminists, but also to the vast majority of decent citizens.

Moreover, basic income is attractive ethically to those such as myself in the Judaic-Christian tradition who are sceptical that material wealth and individual liberty are the most important things in life, sceptical that personal freedom to amass wealth is an absolute right, and sceptical that a nation has to become wealthy before it can afford welfare. Basic income re-embodies the alternative Biblical assertion that justice for the poor is the basis for, not the by-product of, material prosperity. Basic income makes ethical sense, as well as ideological sense and common sense.

The Reasons Why Not

If there are so many reasons for basic income, reasons upon which both ordinary citizens and political ideologues could unite, why does not everyone vote for basic income? In each section of Chapter Six I presented the contrary arguments, some of which I have indicated to be more important than others. Before locating basic income on the political map it is necessary first to recapitulate the main objections.

In the UK it is striking that those who attend seminars on basic income largely represent the 55% of Britons who do not have a paid job, while employers' organizations and employees' unions are largely absent. Why are those involved in the world of paid labour usually less than interested in basic income? Though many may find it difficult to dispute that basic income makes real the right to earn (because income from other sources will always mean a net gain), they are still uneasy because a full basic income also offers more people than at present a right not to earn. They find that unsettling. The idea that economic security is the basis for, as well as the product of, personal enterprise and hard work seems to turn cherished beliefs upside down. Although a major argument for basic income is that it would help promote productive work and enterprise, it still seems less than credible for many. The dignity and the necessity of labour have gone together since the industrial revolution, and people today find it hard to believe that you can remove the necessity yet retain the dignity.

The chief stumbling block is that basic income is *unconditional*. It does not require the able-bodied adult to be either earning (as do tax exemptions) or seeking paid work (as does welfare). Basic income is therefore believed to undermine the basic institution of industrial society: paid employment. The current social contract is that able-bodied adults (especially males) engage in full-time paid work, and use their earnings to support both their dependent family members and (through taxes) non-kin who are unable to work because of age, infirmity or involuntary unemployment. A basic income would enable able-bodied males to work only part-time or only occasionally and so opt out of their part in this contract. Some argue this would be highly undesirable.

By merging the tax benefit systems into one, basic income blurs the distinction between earners and dependents. Those who wish to maintain the industrial ethic of full-time male paid employment, therefore, often propose the opposite reform of *separating* tax and benefits. They agree that many of our current problems (poverty traps, bizarre incentives, etc) arise from the unco-ordinated overlap between the two systems, but claim these could be better eliminated by separating, rather than integrating, the two systems. One such possibility for the UK[4] would be to increase child benefit, raise the level at which income tax is paid so that no social security recipients have to pay tax, lower the initial rates of tax, and impose a national minimum wage. Like basic income, this would ensure that it is always worth taking paid employment and would increase the net income of the low paid. It would restore the dignity of labour but, unlike basic income, it would not give able-bodied adult males the choice to opt out of paid employment. Further, help can be better directed to where it is really needed. In the USA, workfare programmes are commonly advocated by both right and left as the way to provide economic security without undermining the work ethic.

Basic income's economic consequences (reducing the labour force, stimulating the black economy) are empirical questions, perhaps resolvable only by monitoring a basic income scheme as it is introduced. The moral question, however, is more fundamental: should paid employment remain the only respectable source of income, status and dignity for citizens in our society? I would suggest that all people are due respect and dignity, whether or not they are able to engage in paid employment.

Related are certain political objections. One is that, because they reduce people to beggars, the value of handouts is rarely maintained; the value of basic income would eventually get eroded or indeed it would only get introduced in the first place at a cut-price. Furthermore, basic income would only be viable if a whole host of cherished tax exemptions and social security benefits were abolished, every single one of which would be fought for tooth and nail by vested interests. Moreover, it would probably arouse opposition from social security and income tax collection agencies, either because of the extra workload during the transitional period or because of a reduced load and staff redundancies afterwards. In the UK, it would require two huge government departments with long traditions and rivalries to amalgamate, or at least collaborate. To justify their separate existences, these two departments have in most countries succeeded in persuading their political leaders that taxation and social security are categorically different beasts. This links with the ordinary citizen's perception of tax exemptions as a reduction in the amount the state steals from his hard-won earnings and much to be preferred to welfare benefits which erode his pride and dignity.

A powerful conjunction of politics, economics and morality is what basic income is up against. If equality, liberty and fraternity are on the side of basic income, the established order is against it. The question is, need it be?

I do not believe so. When we move from ideology and political philosophy to the real world, the question is this: how to reform the modern state so that it can ensure economic security for citizens without at the same time inducing dependency in those helped, paternalism in officials and cynicism all round? When this question is asked, a well designed basic income scheme appears as a common sense part of the answer.

A map of ideologies

It may be helpful to locate proponents and opponents on a map of political philosophy (Figure 1)[5]. In my map, there are four magnetic poles of attraction, each representing a pure position of political ideology: 1) *Hierarchy*, or the established order. Historically, this was challenged in the eighteenth century Englightenment by: 2) *Liberty*, or 'liberalism' in the nineteenth century sense of the word, stressing the personal liberty of the individual, the free market and (sometimes) equal opportunity, and: 3) *Equality*, or egalitarianism, stressing equality of outcome and the role of the state in fostering this. The classic battle between Liberty and Equality has (not surprisingly, perhaps) failed to produce a clear winner. In the late twentieth century, disillusion with this tired debate has spawned an alternative: 4) *Ecology*, the small-scale, decentralized, personal society in which needs are better met than in state egalitarianism and in which the unfettered economic activity of the classic liberal is restrained by the limits to growth imposed by nature. We would colour Hierarchy purple, Liberty blue, Equality red, and Ecology green.

There is a chronological dimension to this, with pre-industrial society being characterized by Hierarchy; with industrial society characterized by the battle between Liberty and Equality; and with visions for post-industrial society often focussed on Ecology. Nevertheless, Hierarchy keeps on reasserting itself; what people now call 'tradition' or 'the moral order' has in fact to do with values that emerged during industrial society: hard work, dependent wives, earnings as a measure of personal worth. All four poles are and will for the foreseeable future remain the ideological driving forces behind modern politics in the West.

Political Ideologies: A Map

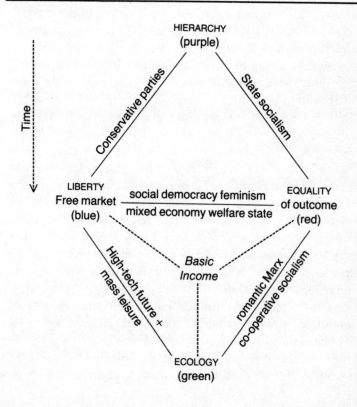

Some actual political parties or movements approximate to one pole. Political rhetoric in USA is often close to the Liberty pole, European Green Parties are pretty near the Ecology pole, and some left wing parties near the Equality pole. But most actual parties and movements have to consider diverse interests and ideologies, and therefore are coalitions, spread out along a line between two poles, with wings and factions trying to pull the party toward one pure pole or the other. They rarely succeed in this, except when hopelessly out of office and able to ignore most of the electorate.

Social democrats are spread out on a line between Liberty and Equality with differing emphases on the market and on state provision at different ends of the line. The welfare state is likewise on this line, with the state restoring a measure of equality where the market has left glaring inequalities, whether in education, health care, housing or income. The Austrian/Swedish 'corporatist' state is on this line, although it has a more integrated vision of equality in relation to liberty. Feminism is also spread out along the Liberty-Equality line, with one wing aiming for a meritocracy and another wing fostering a more socialist vision.

The UK Conservative party and the US Republican party are located along the Liberty-Hierarchy line, with one wing stressing hierarchical values such as 'family' and 'law and order', and the other wing stressing a free market fettered only by minimal law and minimal government. The welfare state is justified by conservatives either in terms of hierarchy, as an extension of ancient paternalism in which the ruling class has a duty to look after the defenseless; or in terms of personal Liberty to enjoy the unequal rewards of the market, as in the Bismarckian notion of social insurance as a reward and incentive for lifelong labour.

Along the Hierarchy-Equality line we find the Soviet-style command economies, strongly centralized and with enforced adherence to the key industrial value of labour.

Below the Liberty-Equality axis we are looking more at visions of the future than at actual major political parties or movements. Along the Blue-Green line we have James Robertson's hyper-expansionist high-tech, high growth future with a few technicians producing the wealth for a mass of leisured morons. Along the Red-Green line we find some of the more romantic passages from Marx and the New Left, the small-scale, co-operative community of Mondragon or certain aspects of Nicaraguan socialism.

Basic income on the map

Where then is basic income on this map? The development of the market (blue) and the state (red) have made it possible for people to free themselves from the hold of hierarchically organized communities and families (purple). Basic income is advocated as the key to a second stage of liberation: freeing people from the oppression of the market or state, or indeed from the unintended new oppressions of the welfare state. This involves a 'greening' of society, not necessarily in the sense of a clean environment, but in the sense of a society (capitalist or communist) in which autonomous activity plays a growing part. Support for basic income therefore tends to come from the lower of the two triangles. In any mixed group discussing basic income, like the Basic Income Research Group or the Basic Income European Network, you will observe socialists trying to pull basic income toward the Red pole, ecologists trying to pull it toward the Green pole, and free-marketeers trying to pull it toward the Blue pole.

There is also support from 'one-nation' Conservatives, at least in the UK. Sir Brandon Rhys Williams MP has been a leading supporter of basic income, Edward Heath when Prime Minister proposed a modest integration of tax and benefits that could have been developed into a basic income scheme, and several backbenchers in the present (1988) Conservative government support integration, including an ex-cabinet minister, Francis Pym[6]. In Holland and Canada, official or semi-official centrist government reports have advocated a partial basic income scheme. All these politicians and others who would normally regard themselves as within the upper (purple-ish) triangle could well join hands over basic income with those in the lower (green-ish) triangle.

Welfare states[7] use taxation and income support to balance up some of the inequalities thrown up by the free market. Liberty is the motor of a free market economy; once the wealth has been created, then attempts must be made to equalize people's lot somewhat. Some early advocates of liberty, however, such as Thomas Jefferson and Adam Smith, understood that — in one sense at least — equality must come *before* liberty. For Jefferson, it was the equal standing of all citizens as landholders that provided them with the liberty to speak their mind; and free market economists since Adam Smith have assumed relatively equal economic actors, a condition that certainly does not pertain today. Advocates of basic income have rediscovered this principle that liberty *depends on* on a certain kind of economic equality, which they believe is best provided by basic income.

Whatever their differences, advocates of basic income, whether they be in the upper or lower triangle, tend to share an understanding that a) a certain kind of equality must *precede* liberty, and b) that renewed efforts must be made to rescue fraternity as a serious political goal.

Chapter Eight

Conclusion

People have become interested in basic income for a wide variety of reasons, many of which I have explored in Chapter Six. There is therefore scope for people of otherwise very different visions to work together on exploring the feasibility of basic income schemes.

Cross-cutting all these approaches are two traditions. Those in the 'basic income' tradition see basic income as the only equitable and efficient way of reforming muddled taxation and welfare systems. The primary aim is to ensure that in an affluent society no one should be reduced to poverty. Some stress the need to end the poverty and unemployment traps, and to foster work incentives for those within these traps. Others stress the need to get money and resources to those needy individuals within a household that as a unit may not be poor. Others stress the need to end the divisiveness of present arrangements which, by treating different classes of citizens differently, foster an impression that some of our poorest, hardest working and loyal citizens are inferior.

Those in the 'social dividend' tradition are concerned that all citizens might truly have a stake in society. We cannot all own a piece of usefully productive land, and it would not help many of us if we could. The dream of each household having a stake in the job market has never lived up to expectations: too many are forced into demeaning work, and many others are excluded altogether. Those without a paid job are abandoned to a life without dignity, or at least to considerable self-searching and guilt; not only unemployed people but also many of us with disabilities, or keeping house, will testify to this.

What is the solution? Experience has shown the socialist dream of state and therefore communal ownership of the nation's property to involve severe practical problems. In any case, in Britain our nationalized industries, in some of which communal ownership does make considerable sense, are being sold off, and one has to wonder whether any foreseeable future government will have the resources to re-purchase them. The capitalist dream of each individual owning shares in private industry is being vigorously pursued in Britain at the moment, but extending significant share ownership will never reach the entire population. Until and unless it does, it will simply lead to a new kind of inequality.

It is in this context of failed solutions and disappointed dreams that some are prepared to look afresh at the problems of life in the late twentieth century. They have begun to ask whether some kind of national dividend, by which every individual citizen owns a share in the national economy and receives regular dividends may not be the way forward. Some socialists see this as the only way to get anywhere near a socialist society in which power is distributed more evenly. Some proponents of people's capitalism realize that a national dividend would redistribute purchasing power to poorer earners and that this is necessary if home ownership and share ownership are to expand much further. Some feminists value basic income as a way of giving women an economic stake in society that many now lack. Some church leaders see a social dividend as expressing the biblical vision of a just society in which all are included and in which all participate responsibly.

These two strands of basic income as a way of preventing poverty and as a national dividend tend to attract different people. But they very much complement one another. It is the strength of the basic income approach to social security that it involves a wider vision of citizenship, dignity and participation. It is not simply a neat technical device, as are so many proposed reforms of social security. At the same time, the concept of a national dividend is not simply a utopian concept, for it can be directly married to the very practical goals of ending the twin obscenities of powerlessness in a democracy and of poverty in an affluent society.

What then is the way forward? To develop the idea of basic income into practical policies that both politicians and electorates will take seriously involves two things. First, there must be wider awareness that there are new ways of approaching seemingly insoluble problems. There must be more informed discussion of basic income, both its philosophy and practicalities, among a wide range of citizens and opinion formers. This is beginning to happen, not least because the idea of basic income has a remarkable capacity to ground discussions of social philosophy in the hard facts and figures of real life, and to leaven otherwise stodgy economic arguments with the vision of a just, participatory and productive society.

Second, hard questions have to be asked if the basic income idea is to be honed down into practical policies. How are wildly varying household costs, such as medicine in the USA or housing in the UK, to be dealt with by a universal basic income for all? If a basic income is intended to meet basic needs, how are these to be defined and by whom? With many presently seeking paid work but finding none, should a guarantee of a basic income be complemented by a guarantee of basic paid work? If so, what implications might this have for individual liberty? For those without paid work, a basic income supplement would probably be required, how are those entitled to this to be identified? Those needing supplements because of disability, sickness or involuntary unemployment will be as difficult to define as at present.

These practical questions are substantial, but no more so than the problems inherent in our present arrangements. They can be tackled if there is the will. Such a will is surely there. There are many who stand firm within a particular political, religious or other commitment, yet who are ready to admit that the problems of the late twentieth century and even of the twenty-first century require co-operation, vision and practical wisdom. If an idea such as basic income cannot inspire the required combination of vision and practicality in people of widely differing parties, then I do not know what else will. The alternative is that many will remain trapped in poverty, with many more trapped into something less than the liberty, equality and fellowship most of us yearn for.

Bibliography

Atkinson, A.B. 'A Guide to the Reform of Social Security' *New Society*, 13 Dec. 1984, pp.426–8. A clear summary and comparison of nine proposed reforms for the UK, including three basic income schemes.

Basic Income European Network Newsletter, Bosduifstraat 21, 2016 Antwerp, Belgium.

Basic Income Research Group Bulletin. Half yearly. From BIRG, 102 Pepys Rd, London SE14 5SG.

Jordan, Bill and Drakeford, Mike 'Major Douglas, Money and the New Technology' *New Society*, 24 Jan. 1980, pp.167–9. Discussion of the implications of Douglas' thinking for post-industrial society.

Jordan, Bill 'The Social Wage: a right for all' *New Society*, 26 April 1984, pp.143–4. Basic income, trade unions and the right not to work.

Jordan, Bill *Rethinking Welfare*, Oxford, Blackwell, 1987. If a basic value is the autonomy and dignity of individual citizens, what should welfare look like?

Jordan, Bill *The State: authority and autonomy*, Oxford, Blackwell, 1985. Wide ranging work of political theory, exploring the free market, socialist and feminist arguments for basic income.

La Revue Nouvelle, No. 81, 1985. Special issue on L'Allocation Universelle. In French.

Miller, Anne *In Praise of Social Dividends*, Dept. of Economics, Heriot-Watt University, Edinburgh EH1 2HT, 1983. Outlines the principles of basic income.

Opielka, M. & Vobruba, G., eds *Das Garantierte Grundeinkommen*, Frankfurt am Main, Fischer, 1986. In German.

Parker, Hermione *Action on Welfare*, London, Social Affairs Unit, 2 Lord North St, London SW1, 1984. Introduction of Parker's BIG options, and comparison with other proposed reforms.

Parker, Hermione *Instead of the Dole*, London, Routledge, 1988. The most detailed study to date of basic income in the UK context.

Purdy, David *Social Power & the Labour Market*, London, Macmillan 1988. The last 3 chapters argue for basic income as a means of developing more equal power relations in the labour market.

Roberts, Keith *Automation, Unemployment and the Distribution of Income*, Maastricht, European Centre for Work and Society, 1982. Advocates basic income as a way of freeing the labour market.

Torry, Malcolm *Basic Income For all: a Christian social policy*, Nottingham, Grove Books, 1988.

Van der Veen, Robert & Van Parijs, Philippe 'A Capitalist Road to Communism', *Theory & Society*, 15, Sept. 1986. Basic income bypasses several of the classic obstacles on the path to communism.

WRR (Wetenschappelijke Raad voor het Regeringsbeleid) *Safeguarding Social Security*, 2 Plein 1813, The Hague, 1985. Argues for a partial basic income for the Netherlands. Free. Dutch and English editions.

USA

There is nothing specifically on basic income published in the USA, but the following three books provide useful background information and discuss briefly credit income tax and social dividend.

Danziger, Sheldon H. & Weinberg, Daniel H. eds *Fighting Poverty: what works and what doesn't*, Cambridge Massachusetts & London, Harvard University Press, 1986.

Garfinkel, Irwin ed *Income-Tested Transfer Programs: the case for and against*, New York, Academic Press, 1982.

Wogaman, Philip *Guaranteed Annual Income: the moral issues*, Nashville, Abingdon Press, 1968.

Notes

Introduction

1. This term was coined independently in Holland in the mid 1970s and slightly later in Britain by Hermione Parker and Sir Brandon Rhys-Williams, M.P.

1. The Crisis

1. Sir William Beveridge *Social Insurance and Allied Services*, London, HMSO, 1942, pp. 6–7.
2. Charles Murray, *Losing Ground*, New York, Basic Books, 1984; Patrick Minford et al *Unemployment: cause and cure*, Oxford, Martin Robertson 1983.
3. *Losing Ground: a critique*, Madison, Wisconsin, Institute for Research on Poverty, Special Report no. 38, 1985; Robert Greenstein 'Losing Faith in Losing Ground' *New Republic*, March 25, 1985. See also Robert Kuttner *The Economic Illusion*, Boston, Houghton Mifflin, 1984; Ramesh Mishra, *The Welfare State in Crisis*, Brighton, Harvester Press, 1984.
4. *Something to Look Forward To*, Macdonald, 1942.
5. Hilary Land, *Women and Economic Dependency*, Manchester, Equal Opportunities Commission, 1986; Jan Pahl, 'Social Security, Taxation and Family Financial Arrangements', *BIRG Bulletin*, 5, Spring 1986.
6. A. Miller, 'Basic Incomes and Women', Louvain-la-Neuve conference paper 1986.

2. What Is Basic Income?

1. See I. Garfinkel, 'The Role of Child Support Insurance in Antipoverty Policy', *Annals* (American Academy of Political & Social Science), Vol. 479, May 1985, pp. 119–131; T. Corbett, 'Child Support Assurance: Wisconsin demonstration' *Focus*

(Institute for Research on Poverty, Madison), 9 (1), Spring 1986, pp. 1–5.

3. Historical Sketch

1. For the earliest origins of basic income in the thought of the Enlightenment, see Edwin Morley-Fletcher, 'Traccia di bibliografia ragionata — I: Per una storia dell'idea di minimo sociale garantio', *Rivista Trimestrale*, Nos. 64–66, Oct. 1980 — March 1981; also E. Bellamy, *Looking Backward* (1988), Harmondsworth, Penguin, 1983.

2. See C. Douglas, *Economic Democracy* (1920), 5th edition, Sudbury, Suffolk, Bloomfield Books, 1974; Jordan & Drakeford (see bibliography); James Generoso, 'Social Credit 1918–1945, An essay and select bibliography', New York, mimeo, 1981.

3. Oskar Lange, 'On the Economic Theory of Socialism' & 'Mr. Lerner's note on Socialist Economics', *Review of Economic Studies*, 5, 1936, pp. 53–71, and 6, 1937, pp. 143–144.

4. *Something to Look Forward To*, London, Macdonald, 1942. See also J. Rhys-Williams, *Taxation and Incentive*, London, William Hodge, 1953.

5. J.E. Meade, 'Poverty in the Welfare State', *Oxford Economic Papers*, 24, 1972, pp. 289–326; *The Intelligent Radical's Guide to Economic Policy*, London, Allen & Unwin, 1975.

6. M. Friedman, *Capitalism & Freedom*, University of Chicago Press, 1962; C. Green, *Negative Taxes and the Poverty Problem*, Washington DC, Brookings Institution, 1967; R. Theobald, *Free Men and Free Markets*, Garden City, Doubleday, 1963, and *The Guaranteed Income*, Garden City, Doubleday Anchor, 1966; *Proceedings of the National Symposium on Guaranteed Income*, Washington DC, Chamber of Commerce of the United States, 1966; *Industrial Relations*, Feb. 1967; Wogaman (see bibliography).

7. D. Coyle & A. Wildavsky 'Requisites of Radical Change: income maintenance versus tax reform', paper given to conference on The Income Maintenance Experiments: Lessons for Welfare Reform, New Hampshire, September 1986. See also D. Moynihan, *The Politics of a Guaranteed Income: the Nixon administration and the family assistance plan*, New York, Random House, 1973.

8. See H. Heclo, 'The Political Foundations of Antipoverty Policy', ch. 13 in Danziger & Weinberg (in bibliography).

9. On credit income tax, see Garfinkel, 'Professor Friedman, Meet Lady Rhys-Williams: NIT vs. CIT' *Jnl. of Public Economy*, 10, 1978, pp. 179–216; K. Keniston and Carnegie Council on Children, *All Our Children*, New York, Harcourt Brace Jovanovich, 1977, pp. 104ff.

10. *Royal Commission on the Economic Union and the Development Prospects for Canada*, Ottawa, Canadian Government Publishing Centre, 1985, ch. 19; *Statistics Canada*, 1986, pp. 28, 144.

11. D. Drake & D. Cameron, *The Other Macdonald Report*, Toronto, James Lorrimer, 1985.

12. *Proposals for a Tax-Credit System*, London, HMSO Cmnd. 5116, 1972.

13. A.B. Atkinson, *The Tax Credit Scheme and the Redistribution of Income*, London, Institute for Fiscal Studies, 1973.

14. C. Sandford et al, eds, *Taxation and Social Policy*, London, Heinemann, 1980, ch. 12.

15. *The Reform of Personal Taxation*, London, HMSO, Cmnd 9756, 1986, para 6.10. Curiously this same document proposes massive tax exemptions for wives who have neither paid employment nor dependents to care for.

16. Parker, *Action on Welfare* (in bibliography).

17. House of Commons Treasury & Civil Service Committee, session 1982/3, *The Structure of Personal Income Taxation and Income Support*, May 1983 (The Meacher Report), paras 13.19–13.35.

18. Philip Vince, '*To each according. . . .*', London, Women's Liberal Federation, 1983.

19. SDP/Liberal Alliance consultative paper, *Partnership for Progress*, London, July 1986, pp. 47–9.

20. Ecology Party, *Working for a Future*, London, 1980.

21. Colin Clark, *Poverty Before Politics*, London, Institute of Economic Affairs, 1977; Patrick Minford, 'State Expenditure: a study in waste', *Economic Affairs*, April — June 1984.

22. Ralph Howell, *Why Unemployment?*, London, Adam Smith Institute, 1985.

23. A. Dilnot et al, *The Reform of Social Security*, Oxford University Press, 1984.

24. See Robert van der Veen, 'Basic Income: the debate in the Netherlands', Louvain-la-Neuve conference paper 1986.

25.   See bibliography for full reference.

26.   Van der Veen, op. cit., p.6.

27.   Gunnar Lindstedt, 'Give Us a Basic Income', *Metallarbetaren*, 45, 1986.

28.   London, Marion Boyars, 1981.

29.   *Partage*, No. 31, Oct.— Nov. 1986.

4.   Who Pays and How Much?

1.   An exception is F. Field, *What Price a Child?*, London, Policy Studies Institute, 1985. See also D. Piachaud, *Family Incomes Since the War*, London, Study Commission on the Family, 1982.

2.   In other words, poverty is relative to the society in which we live; see W.G. Runciman, *Relative Deprivation and Social Justice*, London, Routledge, 1966; R. Holman, *Poverty*, Oxford, Martin Robertson, 1978. Peter Townsend notes that mere physical subsistence, without our being able to fulfil social obligations, makes life not worth living; poverty, therefore, is a standard of living so low that I am not able to fulfil normal social and economic obligations to family, friends and neighbours. (Townsend, *Poverty in the United Kingdom*, Harmondsworth, Penguin, 1979, and Townsend, ed, *The Concept of Poverty*, London, Heinemann, 1970.) Unless we are to regard humans as non-social animals, the poverty line will rise as affluence rises.

3.   Jeremy Seabrook, *Unemployment*, London, Quartet Books, 1982, p.3. Both Seabrook and Ivan Illich eloquently describe in their books this loss of the ability to do things for ourselves without cash. J. Gershuny in *After Industrial Society?*, London, Macmillan, 1978, describes the apparently contrary trend of doing-it-yourself because of the ever increasing cost of paying someone else to do it, but both he and Ray Pahl, *Divisions of Labour*, Oxford, Blackwell, 1984, stress that nowadays you need money even to do it yourself. Power drills and home sewing machines may be cheaper than other people's labour, but they are not free.

4.   This raises difficult and important questions about the relation of basic income schemes to Third World development, and about the dubious pursuit of happiness through materialism. These are touched on in Wogaman (in bibliography) pp. 124–8, and in my own *All You Love Is Need*, London, SPCK, 1985 (published in USA as *Need: The New Religion*, Downers Grove, Inter Varsity Press), ch. 3.

5. Further details are in Parker, *Action on Welfare* and *Instead of the Dole*, and *BIRG Bulletin* No. 3, Spring 1985.
6. There is debate about how to cost this kind of basic income scheme. See A.B. Atkinson, *The Cost of Social Dividend and Tax Credit Schemes*, ESRC Programme on Taxation, Incentives and the Distribution of Income Discussion Paper No. 63, April 1984; H. Parker, 'Costing Basic Incomes', *BIRG Bulletin*, No. 3, 1985; 'The Debate About Costings', *BIRG Bulletin*, No. 4, 1985.
7. *Capitalism and Freedom*, University of Chicago Press, ch. 10.

5. The Incentive To Work

1. J. Rhys-Williams, *Taxation and Incentive*, London, William Hodge, 1953, pp. 125–6.
2. C.V. Brown, *Taxation and the Incentive to Work*, Oxford University Press, 1983.
3. 'Basic Income: a basis for small business', Louvain-la-Neuve conference paper 1986.
4. 'Basic Incomes and the Elderly', *BIRG Bulletin*, No. 6, Autumn 1986, pp. 5–10.
5. J.A. Pechman & P.M. Timpane, *Work Incentives and Income Guarantees: the New Jersey Negative Income Tax Experiment*, Washington DC, Brookings, 1975; SRI International, *Final Report of the Seattle-Denver Income Maintenance Experiment*, 2 vols, 1983.
6. pp. 798–9.
7. See H. Parker *Costing Basic Income*, UK, Louvain-la-Neuve conference paper, 1986, p. 8.
8. P-M Boulanger, 'Stimulating Impact of Basic Income on the Belgian Labour Market', Louvain-la-Neuve conference paper 1986.
9. R. Pahl, *Divisions of Labour*, Oxford, Blackwell, 1984, p. 336. See also Tony Walter, *Hope on the Dole*, London, SPCK, 1985, chs. 5 & 11.
10. R. Titmuss, *The Gift Relationship*, Harmondsworth, Penguin, 1970.
11. See Bill Jordan, *Rethinking Welfare*, Oxford, Blackwell, 1987.

6.i. Simplicity

1. This example is from Howell, *Why Unemployment?*, op. cit.

6.ii.   Preventing Poverty

1. A. Dilnot et al, *The Reform of Social Security*, Oxford University Press, 1984.
2. Jan Pahl, 'Social Security, Taxation and Family Financial Arrangements', *BIRG Bulletin*, No. 5, Spring 1986.
3. Lawrence Mead, *Beyond Entitlement: the social obligations of citizenship*, New York, Free Press, 1985. Quote from Danziger & Weinberg, eds, (in bibliography), pp. 285–6.
4. T.H. Marshall, *Citizenship and Social Class*, Cambridge University Press, 1950.
5. *BIRG Bulletin*, No. 6, Autumn 1986, p.8.
6. P. Wogaman, *Guaranteed Annual Income* (in bibliography), p. 84.
7. H. Heclo, 'The Political Foundations of Antipoverty Policy', in Danziger & Weinberg, eds, (in bibliography), p. 337.

6.iii.   Two Ethics

1. See Wogaman (in bibliography) for a good discussion of the ethics of various guaranteed income schemes. For a general discussion of citizenship, see T.H. Marshall, *Citizenship and Social Class*, Cambridge University Press, 1950.
2. *Fair Shares?*, Edinburgh, Handsel Press, 1985, ch. 3.
3. Quoted in R. Bellah et al, *Habits of the Heart*, Univ. of California Press, 1985, p. 260.
4. Marx, I think, understood this dual relation. The vast increase in production in his time he saw as the result of accumulated 'dead labour' by past workers, present in current technology owned by the capitalist. Hence the capitalist appropriates both surplus value from his present workers plus the fruits of past surplus value in the form of advanced technology. Marx's concern, of course, was that prosperity goes in large measure to the capitalist rather than to the working class whose labour, past and present, is its source.

    In the longer term, Marx foresaw this mass of accumulated 'dead labour' as capable of production without the labour of the current working class, in other words automation-induced unemployment (*Grundrisse*, Harmondsworth, Penguin 1973, p. 705). Presumably what matters from this point on is that the fruits of 'dead labour' get siphoned back to the current working class by some mechanism; would Marx have approved of basic income? I explore this question of automation in the following section.

5.   I have explored this in detail in *All You Love Is Need*, London, SPCK, 1985 (published in USA as *Need: the new religion*, Downers Grove, Inter Varsity Press); 'The Politics of Grace', *Third Way*, Nov. 1986, pp. 10–12. Some possible reasons for the different experience of scarcity in African and Anglo-American peoples are suggested in my 'Children of Africa', *Resurgence*, 119, Nov/Dec. 1986. See also W. Brueggemann's *The Land*, London, SPCK, 1977, and Bellah et al, *op. cit.*

6.   M-L Duboin, 'Guaranteed Income as an Inheritance', Louvain-la-Neuve conference paper 1986.

7.   Basic Income For All: A Christian social policy, Nottingham, Grove Books, 1988. See also Malcolm Torry 'Realistic Radicalism' BIRG Bulletin, 5, Spring 1986; Wogaman (in bibliography), ch. 3; Tony Walter, *Fair Shares?*, op. cit., chs. 3, 7, 11; 'Salvation and Work' *Faith and Thought*, 106, 1980, pp. 135–150.

8.   See Hermione Parker, *The Moral Hazard of Social Benefits*, London, Institute of Economic Affairs, 1982; and *Instead of the Dole*, in bibliography.

9.   In a letter to the author, February 1987.

10.   See the following section on automation.

6.iv.   Automation

1.   Recent studies of the effects of automation are J. Keane & J. Owens, *After Full Employment*, London, Hutchinson, 1986; C. Gill, *Work, Employment and the New Technology*, Oxford, Polity Press, 1985; and more optimistically A. Francis *New Technology at Work*, Oxford University Press, 1986.

2.   *The Sane Alternative*, Ironbridge, 1983, and St. Paul, River Basin, 1980.

3.   C. Handy, 'The Challenge of Industrial Society', in S. Reedy & M. Woodhead, eds, *Family, Work and Education*, Hodder/Open University Press, 1980. See also Kurt Vonnegut's SF novel, *Player Piano*, London, Macmillan, 1953.

4.   A.G. Watts, *Education, Unemployment and the Future of Work*, Milton Keynes, Open University Press, 1983, p. 124.

5.   See the articles by Smail in *BIRG Bulletin* No.4 and Vince in *BIRG Bulletin* No. 5.

6. André Gorz, 'L'Allocation Universelle: version de droite et version de gauche', *La Revue Nouvelle* 81, pp. 419–428; Robertson, *Sane Alternative*, op. cit. pp. 83–4. Niels Meyer (*Revolt From the Centre*, London, Marion Boyars, 1981) and Gunnar Adler-Karlsson also envisage basic income as part of a left-ecological society.

7. In R. Theobald, ed, *The Guaranteed Income*, Garden City, Doubleday, 1965, pp. 175–184; quote from p. 183.

8. Bill Jordan, *The State* (in bibliography), p. 186.

9. *Hope on the Dole*, London, SPCK, 1985.

10. See Keane & Owens, op. cit.

6.v. Liberty

1. See for example M. Friedman, *Capitalism and Freedom*, op. cit.; M. & R. Friedman, *Free to Choose*, London, Secker & Warburg, 1980; F.A. Hayek, *The Road to Serfdom*, London, Routledge, 1976.

2. Jordan, *The State*, p. 286.

3. P. Minford, 'State Expenditure: a study in waste', *Economic Affairs*, April–June 1984.

4. *Free to Choose*, pp. 120–126; *Capitalism and Freedom*, ch. 12; and 'The Case for the Negative Income Tax: a view from the right', pp. 111–120 in J.H. Bunzel, ed, *Issues in American Public Policy*, Englewood Cliffs, Prentice Hall, 1968. Minford also proposes negative income tax as part of his 'lowered floor' package.

5. See Roberts for the classic defense of basic income on these grounds; also WRR, p. 61. (Both in bibliography.)

6. The adjustment of the pension age and the moral tagging of those who retire 'early' or work 'late' is documented in C. Phillipson, *Capitalism and the Construction of Old Age*, London, Macmillan, 1982.

7. For the classic left-wing American analysis, see F. Piven & R.A. Cloward, *Regulating the Poor*, London, Tavistock, 1972/New York, Pantheon, 1971.

8. Ferdinand Mount, *Property and Poverty*, London, Centre for Policy Studies, 1984.

9. For a left-wing critique, see Robin Smail 'A Two-Tier Basic Income and a National Minimum Wage', *BIRG Bulletin*, 4, Autumn 1985, pp. 15–17. See also the next two sections, on equality and on women.

10. *Why Unemployment?*, op. cit.
11. See Gunnar Myrdal, *An American Dilemma*, New York, Harper, 1944.

6.vi.   Equality

1. Bill Jordan, *The State*, chs. 16 & 17; 'The Social Wage' (in bibliography). R. van der Veen & P. Van Parijs, 'A Capitalist Road to Communism', *Theory & Society* 15, Sept. 1986, and 'Universal Grants Versus Socialism: Reply to Six Critics', *Theory & Society* 15, March 1987. Claus Offe, *Disorganised Capitalism*, Oxford, Polity Press, 1985. Gerald Roland, 'Why Socialism Needs Basic Income, Why Basic Income Needs Socialism', Louvain-la-Neuve conference paper 1986. David Purdy, *Social Power & the Labour Market*, London, Macmillan, 1988.
2. 'The Claimants Union and the Fight to Live', undated, probably early 1970s.
3. Paul de Beer, 'A Radical Middle Course for Social-Democracy', Louvaine-la-Neuve conference paper 1986.
4. Details in bibliography.
5. Quoted in R. Walker et al, eds, *Responses to Poverty: lessons from Europe*, London, Heinemann, 1984, p. 185.
6. See Hilary Land, 'The Mantle of Manhood', *New Statesman*, 18/25 Dec. 1984, p. 17.
7. *The State* (in bibliography), pp. 320–3.
8. The issues are described in F. Field, *The Minimum Wage*, London, Heinemann, 1984.
9. See for example Smail, op. cit; and P. Vince in *BIRG Bulletin*, No. 5, Spring 1986.
10. WRR (in bibliography) p. 48; verbal statement by Douben to Louvain-la-Neuve Conference, 1986.
11. 'Mantle of Manhood', op. cit.
12. Ibid.
13. For an account of this in West Germany, see Heiner Geissler, *Die Neue Soziale Frage*, Freiburg, Herder, 1976; in Britain, I. Clemitson & G. Rodgers, *A Life to Live: beyond full employment*, London, Junction Books, 1981. A classic debate of the problem as seen by the left in the USA may be found in *The Nation*, 1986; S. Aronowitz 'The Myth of Full Employment', Feb. 8; M. Harrington, 'Progressive Economics for 1988', May 3; F. Block

et al, 'The Trouble With Full Employment', May 17; D. Gordon & S. Brown, 'Vox Pop', Oct. 4.

14.   'A Revolution in Class Theory', *Politics & Society*, 17, 1987.

6.vii.   An Independent Income For Women

1.   See J. Rhys-Williams *Taxation and Incentive*, London, William Hodge, 1953, pp. 145–9; Anne Miller, *In Praise of Social Dividends* (in bibliography), and 'Basic Incomes and Women', Louvain-la-Neuve Conference paper 1986; Bill Jordan, *The State*, Oxford, Blackwell, 1985, pp. 136–9; Hermione Parker, *Action on Welfare* (in bibliography).

2.   Jordan, *The State*, op. cit., pp. 9–10.

3.   Miller, 'Basic Incomes and Women', op. cit.

4.   *Taxation and Incentive*, op. cit., pp. 148–9.

5.   Tony Walter, *Hope on the Dole*, London SPCK, 1985, pp. 105–7.

6.   Carol Brown, 'Mothers, Fathers and Children: from private to public patriarchy', pp. 239–267 in Lydia Sargent, ed, *Women and Revolution*, Boston, South End Press, 1981.

6.viii.   An Independent Income For Those Needing Care

1.   See Bill Jordan, *Rethinking Welfare*, Oxford, Blackwell, 1987, ch. 12; Miller, 'Basic Incomes and Women', op. cit.

2.   'Implications of Basic Income for People with Disabilities', *BIRG Bulletin*, 7, Spring 1988; *Poverty & Disability: Breaking the link*, London, Disability Allowance, 1987.

6.ix.   Social Cohesion

1.   *Communication and Social Order*, Oxford University Press, 1968, p. 137.

2.   See P. Golding & S. Middleton, *Images of Welfare*, Oxford, Martin Robertson, 1982; Tony Walter, *Hope on the Dole*, London, SPCK, 1985, ch. 4.

3.   Haddon Willmer, 'The Politics of Foregiveness', *The Furrow*, April 1979; Tony Walter, 'The Politics of Grace', *Third Way*, November 1986.

4.   J. Coleman, 'Income Testing and Social Cohesion', ch. 3 in Garfinkel, ed, *Income-Tested Transfer Programs* (in bibliography).

5.   I am indebted to Robert van der Veen for much in this section.

6.   Michael Rustin, 'The Non-Obsolescence of the Right to Work', *Critical Social Policy*, 18, Winter 1986–7, pp. 8–14.

7.   Hannah Arendt, *The Human Condition*, University of Chicago Press, 1958, p. 48.
8.   E.P. Thompson, 'Time, Work Discipline and Industrial Capitalism', *Past & Present*, 38, 1967, pp. 56–97, describes the loss of this personal control over one's work and its historical origins.
9.   London, Chatto & Windus, 1984, quote from p.18.
10.   Rustin, op. cit.
11.   'Alternative National Budget for Denmark, including a basic income', Louvaine-la-Neuve conference paper, 1986.
12.   Barbara Ehrenreich, *The Hearts of Men*, New York, Anchor/ Doubleday & London, Pluto, 1983.
13.   R. Bellah et al, *Habits of the Heart*, University of California Press, 1985.

7.   Ideology

1.   Bill Jordan, *The State* (in bibliography).
2.   Theobald, *The Challenge of Abundance*, New York, Mentor, 1962, p. 92.
3.   James A. Yunker, 'The People's Capitalism Thesis: a skeptical evaluation', *ACES Bulletin*, 24(4), Winter 1982, pp. 1–47.
4.   Suggested to me by Fred Twine as a package uniting the Low Pay Unit's national minimum wage proposal and the Child Poverty Action Group's case for raising child benefit.
5.   My map draws on D. Coyle & A. Wildavsky's analysis of American politics, op. cit.; and J.O. Andersson's map of W. European politics, 'Basic Income in a Blue-Green Society', Louvain-la-Neuve conference paper, 1986.
6.   *The Times*, Oct. 16, 1985.
7.   For the alternative corporatist model of Austria, see R. Mishra, *The Welfare State in Crisis*, Brighton, Harvester, 1984, chapters 4 and 6.

National Contacts and Archives

BELGIUM:	Collectif Charles Fourier, c/o Philippe van Parijs, ECOS, Place Montesquie 3, B–1348, Louvain-la-Neuve.
BIEN:	Basic Income European Network, Bosdvifstraat 21, 2018 Antwerp, Belgium
EIRE:	Rosheen Callender, Research Dept. ITGWU, Liberty Hall, Dublin 1.
ITALY:	Edwin Morley Fletcher, Via Bacina 34, Roma.
NETHERLANDS:	Robert Van der Veen, Economisch Seminarium FSW, Herengracht 528, 1017 CC, Amsterdam.
SCANDINAVIA:	Niels Meyer, Technical University, Physics Laboratory, 2800 Lyngby, Denmark.
UK:	BIRG, 102 Pepys Rd, London, SE14 5SG.
USA:	Irwin Garfinkel, Institute for Research on Poverty, University of Wisconsin, 1180 Observatory Drive, 3412 Social Science Building, Madison, WI 53706.
WEST GERMANY:	Michael Opielka, Wiedenschall, 5202 Hennef 41.

INDEX

Adler-Karlsson, Gunnar 32, 87, 93
AFDC (USA) 64
Ashby, Peter 30
Atkinson, A.B. 60
Austria 12, 69
automation 88–94, 164–5
autonomy 7–8, 68–72, 92, 151
  see also liberty

Basic Income Guarantee 1(a)
  40–7, 100, 112, 113, 125–6
Basic Income European
  Network (BIEN) 33, 170
Basic Income Research Group
  (BIRG) 9, 30, 170
basic income supplements 18,
  40
basic needs, see needs
Belgium 19, 33, 170
Bellamy, Edward 93
Beveridge, Sir William 11, 25, 35–6
Bevin, Ernest 113
Boulanger, Paul-Marie 54
Brown, Carol 123

Canada 19, 24, 27–8, 66
Carnegie, Andrew 78, 105
charity 55–6, 97
child benefit (UK) 19, 73, 146
child care 119, 128–20

Child Poverty Action Group
  (UK) 73
children 18, 128–29
Christian social thought 31, 81–2,
  145, 154
citizenship 81–2, 154
claimants 133–6
Claimants Union (UK) 30, 108
class conflict, see social class
Collectif Charles Fourier 33, 170
collective bargaining 96, 108,
  110–4
commodification 36–8
Conservative Party (UK) 31,
  149–51
cost of living, see needs
cost of basic income
  schemes 34–47
Credit Income Tax (USA) 25

Dalton, Hugh 111
Denmark 19, 32, 66
dependency 7, 15–16, 44, 68–69,
  148
disability 129–31
Douben, N.H. 112
Douglas, Major Clifford 23–4, 81
dual-selector economy 89–91
Duboin, Marie-Louise 81
Duncan, H.D. 132

Earned Income Tax Credit (USA) 26–7
earnings, see also wage 15, 70, 77–79, 92–3, 132
ecology, see Green Party
education 13, 67, 100
Ehrenreich, Barbara 140
employment
  creation 74
  full 16
  levels 48–56
  moral virtue of, see work ethic
  part-time 50, 90, 96, 121
  self-employment 51
  women's 49–51, 96, 118–121
enterprise 85, 146
Enterprise Allowance Scheme(UK) 19, 51
equality 84, 107–27, 148–52
ethics 78–87, 145

family credit (UK) 64
Family Income Supplement (UK) 70
family
  allowances 111, 113, 124 (see also Child Benefit)
  break-up 98–9, 125–6
  relationships 116–8, 128–31, 139–40
fellowship, see fraternity
feminism 123–5, 142–5, 150
Finland 36
food 38
food stamps (USA) 26, 64
fraternity 82, 132–41, 152
freedom, see liberty
free market, see labour market
Friedman, Milton 25, 46, 64–5, 98, 102

Fromm, Erich 91

gift 78, 82, 84, 139
Gorz, Andre 85, 91, 93
Green Party 30–1, 33, 150
guaranteed annual income 25–7
guilt 133

Handy, Charles 89
health care 26–7, 36
Heath, Edward 151
Heclo, Hugh 76
hierarchy 148–52
Holland, see Netherlands
housework 16
housing costs 36
Howell, Ralph MP 104

Ignatieff, Michael 139
incentives 48–56, 122, 126
income support (UK) 6, 64
income-tested benefits, see social assistance
incrementalism 66
individualism 140–1
industrial society 14, 142
Institute for Fiscal Studies (IFS) 31, 64–5
Ireland, Republic of 36
Israel 14, 86

Jefferson, Thomas 14–15, 142–4, 152
job-sharing, see work
Jordan, Bill 30, 81, 91–3, 111, 113, 130, 134
Jubilee legislation 14–15

Kennedy, Edward 78
Keynesianism 24

Kuiper, J.P. 31

Labour, see employment/work
  flexibility 91, 100–1
  market 95–109
  Party (UK) 31
  Party (Netherlands) 32
land 14, 142
Land, Hilary 113
Lange, Oskar 24, 81
Liberal Party (UK) 30
liberty 46–7, 85–6, 95–106, 116–
  27, 139, 142–4, 148–52

MacDonald Commission
  (Canada) 27–8, 32, 35, 37,
  53, 74
McGovern, George 27
maintenance payments 62–3,
  69–71
Marx, Karl 107, 109, 149, 151
materialism 86, 136
Mead, Lawrence 74
Meade, James 25, 48, 74
Medicare, see health care
Medicaid, see health care
medical costs, see health care
Meyer, Niels 32, 139
Miller, Anne 15, 30
Minford, Patrick 12, 103
minimum wage, see national
  minimum wage
Murray, Charles 12, 45, 66, 97,
  103

national dividend, see social
  dividend
National Health Service 13, 67
national minimum wage 31, 72–
  3, 91, 97, 104, 111–2, 146

National Union of Students
  (UK) 31
needs 35–8, 84–5, 107–10
negative income tax 20–2, 26,
  27–8, 31, 64–5, 98, 103
  experiments (USA) 52–3, 120
Netherlands 15, 19, 31–2, 66, 75
Netherlands Scientific Council
  for Government Policy
  (WRR) 32, 35, 75, 90, 112
Nooteboom, Bart 51
Norway 32

old people, see retirement/
  pensions
Old Testament 86

Pahl, Ray 55
Parker, Hermione 29–30, 35, 37,
  40–7, 83, 130
patriarchy 116, 123, 139
peasant society 14, 78, 104, 142
pensions, old age 51, 59–60, 64,
  66, 75, 92, 104, 132
political obstacles to basic
  income 48, 147–52
Poor Law (UK) 64, 66
post-industrialism 17, 88–94
poverty 20, 62–76, 98, 135
  relative definition of 37
  trap 49, 111
property 78, 84–5, 103, 107,
  142–4
Pym, Francis 152

Republican Party (USA) 150
retirement age 100, 130–1, 138
reverse income tax, see negative
  income tax
Rhys-Williams, Sir Brandon 29, 151

Rhys-Williams, Lady Juliet 13, 25, 48, 74, 117
rights 12, 74, 92
Roberts, Keith 30, 112
Robertson, James 89, 91, 151

scarity 79–80
school leaving age 101, 138
SDP and Liberal Alliance 30
shalom 86–7, 101–2
single parents 68–72, 125–6, 134, 137
small businesses, see employment (self)
Smith, Adam 101, 152
social assistance 6, 64–5, 119, 125
social class 89, 107–10, 114–6
social credit 23–4, 81
social democracy 149–50
Social Democratic Party (UK) 30
social dividend 19, 24–5, 80–2, 153–4
social harmony, see fraternity
social insurance 26–7, 63–4, 150
social isolation 138–41
social security 6, 39, 63–4, 83
fraud 135
socialism 107–115, 142–4, 149–1
stewardship 78
stigma 65, 132–6
supplementary benefit (UK) 6, 69
Sweden 12, 32, 36
Switzerland 19, 66

targetting of benefits 68
tax 77, 96, 102–3

allowances 39–2, 63, 117, 126, 147
credit 19, 28–29, 63
expenditures 39, 43–4
fraud 135
marginal rates 6, 40–2, 48–49
Theobald, Robert 31, 143–4
Torry, Malcolm 82
trade unions 32, 96, 99, 108
objections to basic income 110–5
Swedish Metalworkers Union 32
TGWU (Ireland) 33
Voedingsbond FNV (Holland) 32

unemployment 16, 33, 53, 96, 99, 104, 133–4
trap 69–72, 119–20
voluntary 92–3
unit of assessment (individual or household?) 20–1, 25, 44, 68, 119–20, 125, 140

van der Veen, Robert 84–6, 110
Van Parijs, Philippe 110, 114
Vince, Philip 29, 30

wages, see also earnings
levels 96–102, 104, 111, 121–2
minimum, see national minimum wage
women's 121–2
Walker, Ian 54
War on Poverty (USA) 25–6
wealth 11, 77–82, 86–7, 101–2
Webb, Sydney & Beatrice 66–7
Wogaman, Philip 76, 164

women, see gender/employment
women's movement, see
  feminism
work
  ethic 15, 17, 77, 83, 105–6,
    136–7, 146
  incentives, see incentives
  sharing 92

unpaid 54–6
workfare 16–17, 74, 104–5
working class, see social class

youth 31, 33

Zimbabwe 67–8